Marginal Copyright ©Grant J. Riley 201

ISBN: 978-0-244-60200-0

To order in paperback please go to www.lulu.com

Also available as an ebook www.amazon.com and in selected booksellers

Other work by the author:

A Journal from the End of Times: On the Trail of the Modern Maya

Also available on www.lulu.com & www.amazon.com

This is a self-published enterprise, for any queries or permissions please email: grantjriley@gmail.com

All names and some places have been changed to protect the author

These stories are dedicated to anyone who has ever tried to do things in a different way.

Acknowledgments:

The inspiration has, of course, been drawn from all those amazing people that I have had around me, on the road. On a more technical and recent note though I need to massively thank Rebecca O'Keefe for her tireless and diligent editing. Thanks for the support and encouragement during the initial proof reads to Nicola Bradshaw and Alexa King. More massive thanks to Ramor Ryan and also to Neil Ansell for their and blurb and invaluable assistance in producing these tales.

Crusties, punks, travellers and squatters, 2000 ravers, together we're the plotters...

You know you know, you gotta go where you shouldn't go...

(Gary DS)

A Day at the Fair

Danny opens his eyes and smells straw. He looks up at the undercarriage of the four wheeler and briefly takes in the intricate, hand-painted tongue and grove. There is a kid furiously feeding on its mother's teat. The nanny goat chewing cud, tolerant in her duty. And then the night before enters his limbo; half-asleep, half-awake, still drunk.

The Jekyll and Hyde, a pub that lives up to its name, upstairs all grand and white; below all dark. There are mirrors set around the upstairs bar enlarging the space, with trinkets on shelves to remind you that you are in the County of Galway.

During the horse fair, to get into the upstairs bar, you need money. Not just money in your pocket, you have got to know money. There is no doubt Danny is in the wrong place as soon as he opens the door. Smoking men bearing pints of stout sternly offer advice, *"You'll be wanting downstairs."*

Immediately stepping backwards Danny reverses quickly down the steps. Away from the grand entrance into an alleyway, and an opposite of the bar above. He steps into the gloom and squeezes into the cramped, candlelit underbelly of this establishment. Everyone is here.

He struggles to piece the night together. He can remember the pool table and some of the banter. The Scratch Man was there again. He was buying everybody drinks - again. Last night's Jamesons linger in Danny's now dry mouth; sour and foul as he pictures the Scratch Man. A strange and slight character, appearing simple... but obviously not. He is dressed badly from a previous decade or two, snorkel coat and corduroys. What's his story? Danny muses. He recalls some tell of tale, his scam and something to do with scratch cards; whatever it was, he is the main suspect in the case of the hangover. Danny doesn't remember having any money, so someone was buying the drinks.

From under the carriage he looks out at the camp. The circle of wagons, the fire pit, the metal food trunks, yog irons, black kettles, the odd bastible and the remainders of children's breakfasts. Danny didn't know what day of the week it was, just sometime in the middle of the fair. It's most probably mid-morning, but he's not sure. The camp seems desolate, maybe most are up and out on their day's business. No doubt one or two are sleeping off a similar night to the one Danny just had.

He is surprisingly comfortable on his bed of straw, dry at least from the outside drizzle, just a few inches from his face. But he is now awake and bodily functions override his comfort and eventually he has to give into his now desperate need to piss.

Danny stares into the graveyard as he relieves himself against its wall. He looks at the tombstones and reminds himself to be grateful — to be alive — but this takes some effort. The enormity of the hangover is increasingly evident; particularly now that he has stood up.

It's strangely quiet up here on this little hillock, up above the green. Down below there are throngs of people and even more horses, the sounds of the fairground are carried by the breeze.

The camp is deserted and Danny has a surge of collective responsibility, as he realises he is the only one here to stand guard. Parked up all around are the Irish Travellers, with their spanking new and plush trailers. Grand china and silver permanently on display. All the seating still in its covers. Danny's lot are somewhat of a bewilderment here, but they have their camp and there is little trouble, for now.

He searches for sticks, water and a kettle in the drizzle. It's now turning to rain. He badly needs some coffee but he is suddenly stopped in his process. Spooked. There is a man. Or is it a ghost?

Alerted he approaches the fire pit and can make out a sitting hunched figure, head down, pulled over by an old tweed coat, staring at the fire; which has long gone out. Danny stoops to try and see the face and he decides, *it's not one of our lot.* As he gets closer he gathers his age - he is old, really old. His face pitted and folded, add on another ten years because they have been spent in the constant winds and rains in the west of this island. His stubble suggests it had been at least forty-eight hours since he last had cared for himself.

"You ok there auld boy?"

No reply.

He is sitting, slouched but very, very still. *"Hey fella... you OK?"*

No response.

Danny goes in close to his face and tries to get eye contact. He is quite a goner, alive, but in another world. The old man begins to mumble and says a few incomprehensible names. Danny decides to return to his own needs for a fire and coffee and proceeds with his chores — one eye on the old man — all of the time.

"What you doing here old-timer?" Danny shouts across the fire pit. *"It's in the wagon, over there."* The old man jibbers. *"Whose wagon, which one?"* Danny replies, reluctantly playing along.

The clarity comes and Danny concludes that this is an ancient traveller back in his old camp. People have parked on this very spot for possibly hundreds of years and this old boy is slipping back between the here and now; his age and a fair bit of drink have him in the twilight.

He is starting to get soaked, so Danny finds a nearby discarded turf sack and gently puts it over the wet traveller's shoulders. At least that'll keep the worst of the west coast rain off him while Danny decides what to do.

I am not going to get this fire lit, Danny thinks to himself as the rain now comes harder. There is no one else around and his mind, body, and soul are all seriously falling out with each other after last night's session. He narrows his attention on the tartan curtain still draped in full over Pat Lacey's open lot. He was in last night's blur, he must still be in the camp.

Danny calls out Pat's name. A groan is returned. *"Pat, let me light your stove and get a kettle on, it's started to lash out here."* A grumbled *g'wan, g'wan*, comes from inside the wagon.

Danny gently pulls the curtain back and quickly finds some kindling to reignite the remainders of last night's embers. Before long the heat finally warms and the kettle comes to blow. Pat continues to groan unseen, deep under his bed covers. Danny sits in the doorway, above the shafts, makes a cigarette and looks out at the figure by the fire.

He goes over and gives the old man a cooling tin mug of tea. Danny puts it in the old man's hands and makes his fingers clasp around the mug. The old man puts the tea to his lips and they start to turn from blue to a more lively grey. Eventually the eyes begin to light and he begins to take in the present. Confused.

Danny has warmed some of last night's stew on Pat's stove and manages to encourage the old man to his feet. It's only a few assisted steps and up over the shafts. Danny could see for this, the old man was well rehearsed. They eat stew and the old man begins to return.

"What's going on?" Hollers the corpse of Pat Lacey, now arisen in his bunk. *"Whad ya doin' wid dat ol'buffer in me wagon, get him out – out! – out!"* He demands in his thick Cork accent. He is none too pleased.

Danny calms Pat quickly and tells him the tale. The soggy old traveller now more compos and aware of his situation.

"You saved me." He looks out into the rain. *"I coulda drowned."* His accent even thicker than Pats.

The old man opens his dog-toothed, woven tweed overcoat and displays his inside pocket. Neatly and tightly tucked inside is a four-inch thick wedge of punts; mainly twenties and fifties by the looks of it. *"C'mon, I'll buy youse a drink for ya troubles."* Danny lifts a smile; the first of the day. Pat groans once more, rolls over and returns to sleeping it off.

Now, being a young fella at this stage, a few of the elders had tipped the lads off on a few do's and mainly don'ts of the Ballinasloe Horse Fair: watch out for bare-knuckle fighters; don't mess with the traveller girls, however pretty they may be; and don't try and get a drink in this pub, or that pub and so on. Tales were told of the year before when a huge family feud had broken out. There were machetes involved, so the stories go, and the Gardaí had simply sealed off the town and left all to get on with it.

The old traveller and Danny now take the short walk to the pub, which is of course at the top of *the don't* list. Danny looks up at the swinging sign and resigns himself to never doing what he is told.

The bar is crammed full with big men, really big men in every sense of the word.

The racket of the banter suddenly stops all at once. Glasses are stamped firmly to the bar.

"What d' feck are ye doin' wi Grandpa?"

Danny is suddenly reminded of his own scrawny, scruffy overall appearance and accompanying stench. A hanging hedge-monkey. At least he has his youthful speed and takes a chance at the door.

But Grandpa grabs his arm and assures the oversized men that he is a guest and quickly tells all the tale. It's not a warm welcome but soon Danny has a drink thrust into his hand. He gulps the creamy, black pint as his headache shifts from agh to ahh. He looks around through his eyebrows as a half pint sups quickly away. He wipes the frothy moustache with his sleeve. *"A Jameson's. No. No ice, thank you."* His eyeballs purr as he throws the double back in one.

Not really part of the room but he finds his space at the end of the bar and relishes the relief as he starts to drink off the night before. The combination of being in the warm and dry and the welcome breakfast drink - today is starting to look up for Danny.

One of the travellers pulls out a huge wedge, also from his inside pocket and cracks it over the edge of the bar. *"Drink!"* he hollers.

Lagers, stouts and whiskies get shared out and then the man sings. It's impressive. It is real and strong and full of stories, not all of which Danny fully understands. This is no karaoke. This is this man's song.

Not long after and another man cracks another equally impressive wedge across the bar and another round of drinks and another song. Equally as powerful. And this goes on. They are soon hammered and Danny begins to feel lucky.

Then they look at him. They know he hasn't got a penny.
"Sing us yer song." Collectively they demand.
"I 'aint got a song." Bleats Danny defensively.
"Sing us yer song." A decibel up this time. *"I'm English, I don't have a song."* He pleads unsuccessfully, as he takes another step down the gang plank.
"SING – US - YOUR - SONG!" They make clear.

Danny is trembling and seriously has no song; frantically he searches and searches his mind for a tune but he can hardly remember the words.

"Back when I was younger they were talking at me. Always yap, yap, yapping and complaining, always m o a n i n g at meeeee."

The song is originally sung in a flat sneer and Danny makes it worse, much worse. The big men wince. By the second verse most backs are turned and awkward conversations are purposefully and noisily returned to. Danny gets quickly drowned out and makes a speedy retreat to the gents.

There is no decision to be made as he slips — unnoticed — out of the back door.

The church bell slowly tolls 12 o'clock midday. Danny starts to think of breakfast and returning to his half-drunk cup of coffee and starts another day at the fair, again.

Ancestor Land

The only thing moving in the murk are the swirls of frozen fog; leaning out from behind the trees, occasionally lurking around a trunk, and at times stretching ethereally across the path. It's probably two degrees below tonight, it will possibly sink another two or more before daybreak. It has been frozen for months amidst one of the harshest winters for years, only intermittingly pausing for a bout of drizzle, otherwise simply raw.

They don't use torches. Sean can see far ahead and all around, never having to adjust his eyes. It is unlikely at this time of night that anyone is in wait, but you never know. And besides, as the time is now getting close, he wants to be able to pitch his night vision against those who might not be able to see in the dark so well. They have been in these woods for nearly six months, so each step is well-rehearsed. And as for torches, they just give you away.

A sleeping pheasant is disturbed. Its' alarm echoes throughout the frozen forest. It doesn't bother them, as this is their land — for now. They are the last people to dwell in these woods. Some of these trees, in their infancy, may have hosted armies of the Civil War giving shelter here and there. Undoubtedly much of this land has watched the comings and goings since the ice retreated; matured yes, but pretty much unchanged. The morphic resonance of this woodland is obvious, especially in the dark. One need not close their eyes and imagine, it is simply just there. This is Ancestor Land.

They have been spread out but eventually gather at the base camp, beneath the almighty Pine. The collective voices are once again rowdy, returning to a similar level of volume as when they had left the town. A few complaints are yelled out from a hundred feet above and jovial obscenities are exchanged. The remainders of a fire still smoulders as Sean stokes it, waiting his turn to get into the tree. As the first flames begin to lick, he looks out over the agonising vista into the night's tenebrosity. The young man squats on his haunches and rubs his hands warm as he ponders the landscape in front of him. Where once stood ancient woodland, now lays mud. Skirmishes have been intensifying over these last few winter months, the Romans ever encroaching. Their empire of dirt expands. Mighty and ancient oak trees are being destroyed without a thought. Their corpses dragged onto pyres, smouldering heaps that last for months.

Their centuries of history lost forever — this Ancestor Land defiled.

You will find it hard to describe your connection to the land, especially to the rationalists. They don't seem to be able to understand the time frame for such a habitat to exist, those millennia past. They can't see that this is all of our heritage and impossible to replace. The practical and conservative, repeat: *We must have progress at all costs*. Growth, they say, is essential and just.

Cancerous, Sean thinks to himself. They would be horrified if I chopped up an antique table for kindling right now, mortified if I had used an ancient manuscript to light my fire. But this landscape, to the pragmatic is disposable. Desecrated forever, without grace.

The fire now rages. Dry and seasoned blackthorn lick with descent flames. These particular sticks have been saved for those coldest of nights.

The sadness and the rage enters his soul once again, as it does when you get a few moments alone. The mud of their progress, featureless and grim. They know they are coming for them tomorrow and Sean is away, deep in his thoughts, as he contemplates potentially his last night here.

He knows they are coming, but only in his bones. There is no real evidence, perhaps by a process of elimination, they are coming to get them next. The weather has held the forces back a few times with heavy blizzards of snow. So too have allies on the mainland, who sabotaged some of their more recent attempts. But now they are coming. They are ready, and so is Sean.

Everyone knew it at the Clock Tower earlier this night. Even Cassey, the landlady, recognised that the time was now. She even gave them a dusty old bottle of mead, which she had been saving for a particular event. She knew it was time, they all knew it was time. They had been some of her best customers over the months, always bringing wise cracks and wild stories along with unusual and plentiful custom. And now it was over. They were bought drinks all night as everyone knew it was going to be their last session in here.

It is at least a few hours walk back to the camp but Sean loved these late winter nights: overland and through the woods; a warmly glow from alcohol and heavy protective clothing - snug and cocooned. Yet he is in need of relieving himself and his frozen finger tips now grapple with the underwear. Top layers of dense weatherproofs cover a pair of thick trousers over long johns, with a harness in between the upper two. The harness never comes off at this stage. To successfully complete a basic need in this attire takes some patience and expertise, to get it wrong in these conditions could mean a seriously uncomfortable night.

A shout comes from above. Sean's long stare at the fire is broken. It's his turn to ascend. First taking a long, slow and very cold deep breath, he then purposefully rises to stand.

Thin prusik ropes are pulled out from under the first layer of trousers. The two strands are not much fatter than a shoe lace. Both are tied to the hanging rope with the very specific prusik knot, one above the other. The top rope is attached to a carabiner on the harness, whilst the other dangles freely for the foot. Each knot tightens around the rope when weighted and is easily undone when the weight is released; theoretically. A few checks and alterations are made. Sean twists and unclips a caribina and moves the figure of eight back to a position out of the way. It had not been adjusted since his abseil earlier in the day. He briefly inspects the aluminium tool as he moves it, and observes deep and worn helical grooves from overuse and simply tuts to himself. Sean stands alone, the last on the ground, just him and the dark of the forest and stares straight up the ninety feet above to a small light shining through a hatch. It's always a long way up and it never gets any easier. The sheer physical exhaustion of hauling your body up over and over again and the fear; the absolute fear. Dangling high above the ground on two thin bits of rope has its risks, and your body's chemistry never lets you forget it. Not for one moment.

Sean sits back in his harness and lowers his total weight to just a few feet above the ground. He bounces for a safety check, makes sure everything is still tied on correctly and — HUUUP — and another — HUUUP. His freezing fingers loosen the top prusik knot as he slides it a mere few inches up the rope, then leans back in the harness once again. Sean tilts and slides his foot prusik a similar distance as the top knot before — and HUUUP. Now standing up, knees straight, one foot held firm in the lower prusik loop. The ale swills around Sean's belly, his abdominals work extra hard. He does not always enjoy this climb, but it is the only way home at this stage. And another — HUUUP.

Shaking and sweating from the sheer effort, yet he is hardly ten feet off the ground.

Eventually, at about fifty feet up there is just the silence of the forest - what's left of it. The smell of pyres in the air and the pain of icy, cold air fill his fully inflated lungs.

In those earlier halcyon months at the end of last summer, this was simply paradise.

A solo Corsican Pine had been found penetrating the canopy of ancient oaks in Redding's Copse. A single raised finger to the world. A completely straight and solid length of timber, that towered over a hundred and thirty feet or more into the sky above this ancient coppice. These woods had been here for centuries, if not forever, always defying the biggest of storms. The pine had even survived '87, but its days are numbered; it is possibly down to its last hours.

Now, it towers almost alone. A few remaining oaks and their occupants remain, the last faithful guards stand close by in this otherwise muddied desert.

The first bough of the pine is at ninety feet. John the Bowman had been drafted in for his services. He expertly attached a fishing line to one of his arrows, fired it over this branch neatly enough for the arrow to drop to the other side and slowly fall back to the ground. A sizable length of rope was attached to the fishing line and hauled up and over, slip-knotted and then tied. Then came the first ascent up high into the Pine.

Once into these primary boughs, a spiral staircase of horizontal branches make good for an excellent clamber. Climb up through another thirty feet of tree and the crow's nest is eventually reached.

At about halfway up this staircase you osmotically breach the semi-permeable membrane of the forest's canopy and meet the sky. From the darkness of Ancestor Land below, up above is all clear and blue. A few more branches further up the staircase a pristine orange and yellow carpet spreads out below. The tops of the oak forest are incredibly smooth and even, reaching out as far as can be seen in every direction. The Pine just so happened to be very much in the middle of this copse. During those early days, the autumn colours offered a spectacular spectacle that very few ever get to appreciate. The unity of the forest community is so strikingly different from this unusual perspective, its magnificent canopy viewed from high up above. By the time the crow's nest is grasped, views all across the Berkshire landscape can be seen. A castle sits on one slight hill, a tower occupies another. The Pine feels equal and mighty.

For now, Sean is more bothered by a wind that joins him. About halfway up the rope, more than fifty feet from the ground below, there is little left to protect him from the frosty blast gathering itself from the north. It blows harder as ice forms on his face. Sinking back into the harness he adjusts a scarf across his nose and chin, all tucked under a black, woollen hat. Sean squeezes his eyes to avoid the worst. His fingers are now completely numb as the wind quickly lowers the temperature even further.

The prusik knots are becoming increasingly impossible to undo. Sean can't feel his hands at all. Don't look down. Never look down. But he involuntary peeks. It's more than just the fear, the chemistry brings up the now curdled alcohol from his gut. He slowly debates the bile in his mouth before he reluctantly swallows, for spit may freeze, something to be avoided at all cost.

The icy blast is starting to make his whole body spin. Slowly at first. He has no choice but to grab the main rope tightly and hug with all his force: knees clenched, chin to fists, feet and rope entwined; as the wind begins to give Sean a most unwelcome twirl. He tucks his face further into his chest, keeping his eyes tightly shut now. It is an extraordinarily silent and private moment; helpless, dangling, spinning - in the total darkness, alone.

Sean does not know how long it lasts. Potentially another near-death experience, the mental state - shamanic. However, he does manage to survive once again. As Jack Frost eventually abates after doing his worst, the brawny and lean Sean has to thrash himself like whips to a pack of huskies. He simply has got to get to the top. There is no choice.

Now focussing on the stove, hopefully that tin of tuna he stashed earlier hasn't been found. Sean concentrates on images of the faces, the fire, and hopefully another drink. The will powers him further up the rope.

Eventually faint voices can be heard and the light grows ever nearer. Finally two pairs of strong hands rapidly lift Sean through the hatch, as if he is a sack of potatoes and before he realises it he is on his feet once more. Sean's head spins.

The Doughnut is an impressive structure and has become rather spectacular over these last few months. A two-storey tree house that wraps itself around the huge girth of the Pine. It sleeps about fourteen like sardines and has wood burning and gas stoves, wall-to-wall carpet, windows, a roof and is almost fully waterproof. An absolute luxury around these parts. Tonight it is crammed. Most familiar, some not. Some on form, some subdued. One man rages as another relaxes. There is even a Guardian journalist crammed in there, decorated by a necklace of cameras. There is lager, whiskey, and ginger wine. A radio crackles further drunken nonsense yet it gives the acknowledgement that they are not entirely alone up here in the canopy, deep in this landscape. Sean is the last one in and closes the hatch behind him.

Scouse is ranting, his voice hoarse. He takes more than his fair share of room as he boils a pan of water on the stove, his dreadlocks regularly smashing his neighbours in the face. His sheer size overwhelms some in these confined quarters.

Shiner offers Sean a beer and catches adrenaline in his glint. This after all is what they have survived and thrived on for months, but even at this late stage, tonight is the big one. They don't know for sure, but collectively they share it. There is something undoubtedly in the air.

The night rolls on as they tuck into their supplies. Soon they will be under siege and they have stocked up but, as usual, they make a fairly hefty dent in what has been retained.

Scouse has finished boiling his bags and now offers Sean a handful. Cod in parsley sauce. Sean knows the routine and gives them a shake and a wipe to dry them before putting one bag in each trouser pocket and another two in his top pockets. They are going up to the crow's nest; there is no comfort up there.

It is a sudden and unwelcome return to the elements, as Sean and Scouse leave the warmth and the company of the Doughnut behind. They each squeeze slowly through the top hatch.

Snow is floating around the tree; it is a little more pleasant than the icy wind from before. The climb is relatively easy, however to fall from here is undoubtedly death. In the dark, drunk and exhausted yet exhilarated, they remain clipped onto safety ropes all the way. The clamber involves navigating around a now fully barricaded tree. Hefty cargo nets droop from boughs full of essentials: firewood, building wood, buckets, nails and more rope. High tensile steel cables are pulled taught connecting to the few remaining oaks. This section of the tree is chockfull; part-decor, and part-deterrent. By sunrise these branches will be full of people.

The very last drops of energy allow Sean to hoist himself up onto the final platform at around one hundred and twenty feet. His arms press up, as his belly slithers across the boards. The pain in his exhausted legs is immense, now forcing them up and into the crow's nest. This was the first structure to be built in the Pine and is simply two wooden pallets positioned and roped together. It has hazel bender poles and a tarpaulin cover. The frontage is open to the elements. The vista is priceless. A red dragon on a yellow flag gives colour to the shelter but little in the way of protection; a present from a former campaign. There is also an Aberdeen Angus hide, which a lucky one gets to shelter under, another cherished gift from the people. But there will be no sleeping tonight.

An old ammo box is tucked under one edge of the tarp. It contains meagre supplies, occasional treats, and a small camping gas bottle. The regulator will be frozen, so Sean administers the regular procedure: to lean over the edge and urinate on the gas bottle, trying not to soak your hands. The warm bodily fluid temporarily heats the gas, enough to light it for just a few moments. Then quickly a small amount of water is heated in a thin aluminium billycan. When the flame goes out — a few moments later — the hot water is then poured onto the gas bottle and the process repeated. This can go for some time, if the temperature is particularly low, but eventually you get a hot cup of tea.

On some of those first frozen mornings they had been caught unprepared. On waking with dry mouths, dehydrated by the cold and the drinks from the night before, tongues had stuck to the rooves of mouths, as refreshment was desperately sought. Ice was all that was on the menu, if you were lucky enough to be able to get any out of the frozen water bottle. Never again, Sean had decided, after sticking ice to his leathery, dry tongue. From then on he always slept with a water container as close to his body heat as he could bear.

Sean and Scouse sit crouched and cross legged staring out into the abyss. From inside Scouse's many layers the old bottle of mead is pulled out, like a rabbit from a hat. Nice one. A cork screw on a string, tied to a bender pole, is pulled out ceremoniously to open the bounty. All mod cons up here you see. To drop such a tool from this height would have very upsetting consequences for all parties involved.

Sean pulls the first of the boil-in-the-bags out of his chest pocket. Its warmth has been invaluable; the ones in his trouser pockets have stopped his bollocks from freezing off. Scouse retrieves one of his own bags and they both simultaneously tear off the corners with their teeth, like cavemen. Tilting their heads back and sucking out the contents of a now lukewarm, processed, yellow and creamy slop - which is simply gourmet up here.

They have been at this for some years now, up and down the land. First there was St Catherine's Hill; the beauty all around, outstanding, even by their account. Another timeless, sacred, and irreplaceable landscape. Glorious old England simply hacked into pieces. The urbanities didn't escape either. London's East End, it's cherished and revered communities were avin' none of it – but also got felled by the same axe. Then they went up north, to the valleys of Stamworth, this is where they first took to the trees. The madness, the ferocity, the complete disregard. Solsbury Hill got it but not without total resistance, the once Fair-mile now disquieted forever. By the time they crossed the border into Scotland, the Picts came down from their hideaways and the people of Pollock stood shocked, as their prehistoric landscape was eaten up before their eyes. What sickness brings this upon these lands? They call it progress, we call it greed.

This night. Full darkness. They are only just a short while away.

They wake the forest by roaring into the dark. Letting the ancestors know, their defiance is exorcized - out into the imminent dawn.

Eventually through the daybreak a picture very slowly emerges, like a black and white photograph developing; pegged out on a line, its fluids draining. They can make out the first signs, as things begin to clear. The boundary silhouettes, the vast mud ahead. Then one white wagon appears, then another, yellow coats begin to spew out of each van. It's impressive, they really have gone to town. Over a thousand fluorescent beings begin to take their place, a mile long circular cordon to protect the scene of their final crime. And then Sean can see it. Their *pièce de résistance* all gleaming white. A dinosaur, a trebuchet, a gigantean machine of malintent. By the time it reaches the mud the daylight gives way and the full spectacle unfolds, one hundred and twenty feet below. The Romans march their beast onto the sludge they had fought so hard to secure. Flanked by ranks of twenty or more, they are now joined by columns of the black and blue. An indecisive sleety drizzle ensues as the wheels turn so very slowly. It is an age before it takes its ready position, a grand ceremony for this obscene beast. The forest eaters are coming in for the kill, their imperialism now turned in on itself. All is temporally silent, just the crunching sound of cattipllars across ancient roots. They should have brought drums and conches to put a finishing touch to the absurd scene.

Sean and Scouse blare their air-horns across the countryside, heard for miles around. *It's us, it's our turn. Everyone is to know.* Up and around the tree the people take their positions, each with their own strategy. And simply and silently wait.

Their tools had been too short at first to reach them in this mighty tree. They had previously sent for loftier contraptions, alas their earlier attempts were regularly thwarted by distant allies on the mainland. Significantly delaying and frustrating them for some time. Eventually they acquired this one, here, now. And it stretches up and up, until it is above the crow's nest. Impressive and equally ghastly. Helmeted Neanderthals at the operations, exchanging abuse on their way up to the top. They swipe the huge banner, the Union Jill, from the very summit of the tree.

Triumphant they wave it as they shout out into the early morning sky.

They eventually return at eye level. Rabid dogs in their cage. They growl and bark and froth, their hatred still astounding, to this very day. Sean is sure they would kill him if they could, but exactly why he is not so sure. It can't be for the wages, because they are so measly. Is it just these kind of people they like to stick to these posts? The deranged and psychotic, *Just doin' my job,* it's always been that way.

Despite the increasing aggression directed at them, they all had long ago agreed that non-violent and direct action was the only way. The activists won't fight back, despite being confronted by knives and saws, their insults, promises, tricks and lies. Sean has grown used to all this; but for them it has become increasingly personal. They hack and they slash at the tips of the Pine's boughs. Greenery falling like giant feathers, slowly to the ground. Some of the people are out far onto these limbs, roped in above and below, equipped with bender whips and frays to slow the onset of their saws.

Molten blue polypropylene clogs the chains on the very hot bars of their now stalling machines. Engines splutter, curses are yelled, and a temporary quiet is restored.

Still a few manage to break through, inevitably they carve their way ever closer, honing in on the trunk. That reserved pot of yogurt, which had been waiting here for six months, is now accurately thrown down the back of the collar of the first Neanderthal to attack. As he swipes forward, the gap between his neck and his boiler suit had become apparent and is now filled with semi-frozen mouldy dairy slop, his retreat hysterical. The next to attack receives a small latex glove filled with a dollop of shitty brown paint. A gentle but constant barrage of these paint bombs is enough to see off the aerial assault and the beast quickly retracts its neck, as its operatives swiftly and desperately withdraw.

Whoops, jeers and cries boom across the expansive opening. Ground support has now arrived in good numbers and further sounds come up from below. Sean clambers the foot ladder strapped to the uppermost tip of the Pine, and gains another fifteen feet above the scenario. A single fist raised high in the sky. He can feel trees crashing around him and down below the last of the ancient oaks are being felled. Their weight, like collapsing elephants, cry so slowly as they smash the ground. Sean feels their death quake all the way up here. Another falling tree hits the side of the Pine, the enormous weight of centuries of steady growth, jolts so severely it nearly throws all out.

They shake the trees in moments like these; manic, primitive, despairing and angry. Sean and Scouse howl. And the wind joins them and they howl some more. The branches shake. And the wind screams even furthermore.

Then there is the most almighty crash. And then screams and shouts and more. They have pushed the last oak tree over and along with it have severed the neck of their prized beast. Not only have they hit their crane, but they have carelessly felled three of their climbers. The men could be badly hurt and the atmosphere now changes. Serious. Silent. Potential death is in the air. The extent of their aggression, now turned inward, taken out by friendly fire, man down.

35

Sean gets back in the crow's nest and manoeuvres to get a better view. At first he sees their now pathetic and mangled wreck of a machine. Contorted and dead under the weight of a five hundred year old oak. He can also see their sheriff, in his red hardhat, callously look up as he continues to eat a sandwich. The rest of the team are a lot more concerned than their sheriff appears and a major rescue ensues. The climbers looked shocked, but seem to have escaped the worst.

The mercenary hired helpers are now carted away, three are stretchered out. It takes time for the chainsaws to retrieve their broken beast. Pitifully and eventually it reverses, an ungainly withdrawal, all heads are lowered. The yellow and blue coats all go home for the day. The scale of this spectacle has been astounding. Their retreat subdued. None of them seem to believe in this, most are just there on the minimum pay. Just another shitty day.

The Pine is the last one standing in this former forest. The only tree that remains upright in these hectares of once Ancestor Land. Remaining defiant, for a little while longer, but nothing, nothing at all, will stand in their way — their progress.

A Wiltshire Conspiracy

A new fire begins to crackle. Light smoke smudges through the canopy as the sun sets.

They don't quite know how they have found each other, but they have, instinctively. Four miles and a bit, just outside of the drawn line, on the very edge of the exclusion zone. Individually they have all snuck their way by hedgerow and have somehow managed to gather here, deep in these ancient woodlands, apparently unnoticed. It is covert, secretive, but essentially all are apprehensive. Some have carried water, some have brought supplies, but quickly and surreptitiously they have claimed their ground.

All begin to settle down. Each whispers to another, until one proclaims: "Why the quiet? Let's not be scared!"

Young punks crack ciders as others gather sticks. The fire is kept small in the hope that their smoke won't be seen.

Gena has made her own way here. Hitchhiked from the east, around London and now here in good time. She sits happily, yet lightly chews her lip. It was only a year ago when she would have just sat the last of her school exams. Picturing herself: sweet sixteen, white shirt, ink stained cuffs, sat in the large examination hall as she day-dreamily bemused over all she had been taught. And now, here, in a diametric uniform. It all seemed so mad to her. The missiles, the threats, the obscenities, and the lies. It wasn't war but a civil divide; and she had definitely made her choices.

Light chat and banter ensues while thoughts and tactics for the night ahead are shared. Soup is passed around and they all break the bread. Each offers their story; where they have come from, why they are there. They talk of the previous year's violence: the truncheoned peaceful, the rounded up children, those dogs shot dead – the continuing horrors of the state unfold. Collective shudders circle around the fire-pit. None of them quite know why they are there, defiance runs thick in their blood. They have to live in this country as well and things are going from bad to worse. The narrative is in riddles - a macho chest beating standpoint, hankering for its imperialist past; its stance is a shock for this next generation coming through. A Cold war, an iron maiden - a tin man with no heart, more like. Bombs for the Russians, batons for the boys whose coal they no longer seem to need; desperately clinging onto those last little islands, at any cost, it now seems. The Empire is hungover and it is not a pretty sight. The sun has set in the West.

The assemblage looks around at each other, a little madness in their eyes. It is so hard to articulate the rage at this stage, especially for those so young. But here they are, thorns in their sides, ready to defy. It's a long night ahead and most are here to spectate, some to provoke, yet no plan is made. Just simply their presence alleviates the felt subjugation and that is the best they will get, for now.

Gena reflects, chuckles to herself, and considers what the hell was she doing here? She had watched events unfold these last few years, gatherings, alternatives - more exciting lives had appeared on the TV screens and filled the headlines each day. But she had been a school girl, firmly held by the rein, and now she was simply... free. Again she questions her position, and wonders why she is here; as moths to the candle's flame. A lump forms in her throat, but she looks up and smiles as she is passed a cup of tea.

Gena holds the white and chipped tin mug. She momentarily stares at the hot, murky contents and gulps an earthy flavoured swig. She gags slightly. A lean, beanpole of a lad with Marc Bolan hair stokes the fire and quickly, yet reassuringly, catches a glimpse of her eye.

The sun makes its last dapple, and slips off quietly and pink. The odd rook caws and a wood pigeon calls it a night. The darkness undertakes its shift.

They all stare into the fire, the hippy TV, as it now gives light to this incumbent night. The chatter's slow, as each are together, yet on their own. Restlessness sets in, tongues tingle, and some slowly get up to explore.

Dank moss, the occasional fern, and woody detritus rot in the air. The solider lies there, arms folded across his chest, his torso laid out flat. Amidst the leaf litter, a young British Private from the

Second, now sinking to the First World War. Below the crisp, dry leaves comes the mulch, where the worms come up to feed. And the soul sinks further towards its past. Middle-aged and medieval, lowered into the topsoil and further down to the clays. Norman, Saxon, Viking. Helmets of steel then bronze; rounded, noses guarded, chain mail and shields. Roman, then Briton, and further Gena transcends into her past; the past. The history of this woodland, ancient and unchanged. Down through the sedimentary layers, further and further until she reaches the bedrock. The cretaceous stone, chalk, bones and skulls. She blends with the diatoms and then the atoms until there is nothing of her left. There is now no doubt, she is part of it all.

Her head rests against the base of an elderly oak tree as she feels comfort on her return. Accepted and fearless, feeling her part of here and now; a smile beams broadly to itself in the dark. She has no idea how long she has been here. Centuries probably, moments maybe? And so she rises, leaf and dust brushed off, and heads back towards the fire.

She hesitates in the half-light — in that no-man's land — just beyond where one can be seen from the fire. Her dreams and the present mix uncomfortably as she makes out a new figure in the group. A radio crackles and bleeps and she thought she saw a small, red light flash. The silhouette is boxlike, oversized and not quite human.

The bean pole lad has now made her out and projects a soft smile towards her. It's OK. She takes one more step forward, and yes it is a squaddie sitting by the fire. He now drinks from the tin mug as he strangely and nervously explains himself. His orders, the game, his disillusionment and his lost youth. The fire dwellers are amused yet wary as he continues his tales of woe: "I'd rather be out 'ere with youse lot, but its orders see." His downhearted West Country accents reveals his true boy, separated from the armoured persona he has begun to train. He reiterates his misery and tells them how shite his army life is. He talks of flashing lights and injections in secret bases and fearing for his life. Gena is not sure how to understand it all, she is not sure if he is really there at all. But she knows the atmosphere has changed. She preferred it out there, on her own. Hankering for the past and that feeling, she slides back off into the woods.

Now moonlit, the tracks of badger and deer illuminate and she easily strolls through the brush, ever so light-footed. Brambles tangle and lay in wait, but her passage is smooth; she is welcome here. Low boughs, stretched limbs, young oak and beech leaves reach out from old trees, besprinkled by the night's light. She is home.

And then as the near full moon rises, the edge of the forest is reached. An eight-foot high steel fence marks the end of her trail. Double barbed wire indicates more aggression than just a local farm, a sign informs it is the land of the state. The Ministry of Defence warns of fines, prison, tanks and bombs. She reads half the sign as she peels off her coat. Is it electric? There is no sign. Without hesitation, nor getting to the end of the notice, or even looking around - the coat has been flung over and covered the nasty barbed wire. An athletic scramble and an army-style gate vault lands her safely on the other side.

Crouched and expectant, the aftermath of that sudden flurry of sound now quiets. All she can hear are the thuds of her heart as she gently retrieves her coat and dons it once again. The *other* side of the fence — so different — yet, just the same. She is now near the edge of the plain where it is ridged, and this she slowly begins to trace; aside the fence - tight all the way. The land gently scoops off below into gullies and forms made from rains past, in this soft landscape; all neatly manicured by rabbit nibbles, but not by much else. Gena can't quite believe the beauty. No man treads here. The flora is abundant, orchids are common, and now appearing are so many signs of life. The irony, oh the irony, she thinks to herself.

Still remaining crouched, she moves slowly along the narrow ridge. The woodland continues protecting her silhouette; unless they are heat-seeking, she knows she will be OK. She feels safe amongst the vegetation and knows the occasional nocturnal rabbit won't give her away, unlike the noisy pheasant, but they are all safely on the other side of the fence, asleep in the woods. She lies, she relishes; it feels ridiculous to be where she shouldn't be, but she is.

The wood now tapers a corner that turns to the south, but she needs to be heading east. Onto her belly she goes, slithering snake-like, her cover from the trees now gone. As she proceeds, the terrain lowers. The night's light increases and the land slopes off towards the plain; both providing more gullies, shadows and places unseen. She darts across open parts and moves cautiously along the sheltered ones. Essentially her route is unknown, and the way ahead has become unclear. Nonetheless, in badger tracks she trusts, and moves on.

A soft, round summit is reached with a white track across its back. Like a gentle rollercoaster Gena goes down and eventually up again, following the undulations of the land. And then another, and some more. Hillocks, mounds, tumuli? At first presumed a geologic formation, but now doubted due to their regularity and curious uniform. She is in ancestor land and she knows it; the centre of ancient sacred sites, and have the MOD kept it all to themselves? This is a tank range, right? But there are no tracks, no signs. Gena lays, belly flat, slunk over the top of the fourth, maybe fifth mound, and wonders, where on earth she is?

And so it goes on, riding the back of this dragon she clambers over mound after mound to get to the front. The fifth is ascended then a sixth is reached, and finally the last. The seventh is twice the height of the former and stands grand, like a galleon's figurehead.

She hesitates, contemplates, and wonders what lies next. The moon shadow covers the dark side of the last climb, it feels colder yet covered and so Gena begins the embrace. She clings to the gentle ascent as a rider to a horse's mane. She slithers her way to the top, and waits before the horizon. She listens, she smells; her anticipation is at its peak. What awaits this neck of monster when she is upon its head?

She does not know how long she lies there, suspended in animation, cheek down to the track. The hull-like formation of the path allows her security. On either side, grasses are longer and ruderals are taller, spread out to each way. She watches the moon sink on this midsummer's night as a light gloom begins to permeate. She hears the judder of distant helicopters and knows she is now so close.

Finally, she crawls slowly to the top and as her head breaches the mound, all is unfolded for her alone to see. The plain, open and flat - reaching as far as one can make out. The vast nothingness lightly lit in purples and charcoal grey. Then there is the centre piece, maybe half a mile away or more. And then there are the searchlights, lighting up the old time piece for all to see. Two helicopters circle in large figures of eight, a ballet, a light show; but for whom?

She is simply too bewildered to know. It is beautiful, mesmerising, dark and light all at the same time. The ancestors look up at the helicopters above, their heads shake in dismay.

And then she can make out dark figures in the crops and the fields below, appearing steadily, one by one. Magnetic in their force, their destination all the same.

Safe in the Arms of St. Agnes

The tall, lean figure starts to run. Three stretched strides that then quickly break into a short and buoyant trot. Long, thick, black dreads taper down the centre of a crisp, white shirt. The arm is raised vertical as the body contorts to the left; the right wrist twisted, as the red ball leaves the hand with serious intent.

Middle stump. Howdat! A perfect Yorker! The red, gold, and green bonnet of the wicket-keeper bounces and then flops as he jubilantly flings himself into the air fully stretched. The appeal unnecessary, as the batsman takes his gaze off the now discarded stump and begins to walk away, head down.

The late summer sun sets between two tower blocks. Its orange ball now diffuse in the evening's pollution. A decelerating jumbo jet bares its undercarriage over the green; its guttural belly groans, down and down and down.

Campo and Custard walk the perimeters of the game and head towards a small and compact traveller site. A rectangle of corrugated iron and scaffolding built off the gable-end of the last terraced house before the green. There is just about enough room to store a truck and two caravans. Dogs bark as Custard pounds the corrugated door.

"Welcome, welcome!" A bespectacled and skinny Jeeves greets the visitors from knee height - as he opens the door and holds two dogs by their collars.

They all kick off their boots as they enter Jeeves' Roma caravan. Campo and Custard make themselves comfortable on black goatskins which coat the hard plastic seats. They look around and take in the contents of this humble home. There is a lot to observe in such a small space. Roma's are chrome trailers; their insides a house of mirrors, bling to the max. Every cupboard and door is covered by engraved and ornate mirrors which enlarge the space significantly, at least visually. This Roma was probably originally owned by Irish Travellers, now transformed into a different flavour: posters for recent demos, flyers for local gigs, stickers from sound systems, the odd bit of wild wood, and a few feathers decorate this unusually displaced itinerant home.

Campo takes in the familiar air of wood smoke, spices, dogs, and a slight scent of old incense.

They all exchange tales - the summer parties, reclaiming the streets, and incredulous gatherings of a scale previously unknown. It has certainly been an eventful year for them all. Resistance was indeed fertile, the momentum immense. Yet, as the glories unfolded, signs of change were in the air. The countryside was harder than ever to live in, with the state's recent legislation now coming into full force. Families were being pushed around, divided, and broken. The imposed new law meant no more than six vehicles could camp together, splitting units that had been together for years. Jeeves holds his hands up, alluding to his surroundings. A gesture to explain the once rolling Roma caravan that is now confined inside a metal box deep in the Big Smoke.

"Lambeth are on the march," explains Jeeves. "Papers have been served on over two hundred properties in this borough alone." That is a lot of people to displace, thought Campo. He contemplates dark days ahead. He briefly envisions the sanitisation, the gentrification, the eradication. They are always attracted to differing lifestyles, as they have so little real culture of their own. They impose themselves on others without realising they destroy what they have come to embrace. A symbiosis, for sure - but of the parasitical kind.

After curry and more tea, Jeeves offers them a tour of the street. He goes on to explain the history of this place: occupied since the sixties; condemned since the thirties; abandoned for unknown previous years; now a vibrant and diverse community providing haven in the otherwise grime. The situation has been complex, housing associations were formed by some, following renovation and a lot of hard work. Electrics were re-installed, rooves fixed, and dereliction converted back to life. Bills are paid, as is some council tax, but each case is different, down to each and every individual choice. Eclectic, artisanal, and autonomous – this is where the creative flourish. After all, these are the artists; those alleged Stormtroopers of gentrification.

U-Roy plays through open windows from bass-bins inside the Rasta Temple. This grand white building sits central in the street, uniquely different to the red brick terraces to its left and to its right. Strong Patois is exchanged on the steps of the building as Red Stripe drinkers exchange views on this warm summer's evening. Jeeves plays his assumed role of tour guide and tells about Bob Marley's several stays here during the 1970's.

All exchange straight-faced nods of recognition as they pass by. The adjacent scrap yard is next on the tour guide's itinerary.

Further down the terraced street different tunes can be heard. More bass, still dub, now techno. And it is into this house they enter.

Campo is the last one in but momentarily dwells on the long steps and enjoys the elevated view of the street. These houses, once built for the servants to Buckingham Palace, are now inhabited by a very different kind. So many types. He childishly smiles as he thinks of Sesame Street, the two not so dissimilar. Perhaps just the steps and the railings are all they have in common, but Campo still likes the image in his mind.

Some folk are sitting on the steps to their houses; curious gargoyles are centred above each and every front door. Italian techno punks with leather jackets and skinny legs in tight black jeans load an old blue and rust Dodge 50 truck. A trio of old Jamaican gents wearing smart shirts and trilby hats joke and laugh. Eccentrics, odd bods, and intellectuals all merge. A jumble sale crossdresser walks by precariously balanced on old, cork platform shoes. Dogs bark as children run; it is all warmly animated. This is late summer and the community are out in their street.

In the house the front room is walled by sound. Huge Russian-looking scooped speakers fill the space; two men tweak knobs behind a mass of cables, wires, and hardware. A new dub enters the airwaves of a pirate. You probably don't need a radio if you live locally, their broadcast fills the street. 303s and subs slack Campo's jaw, he involuntary gurns, the music's effect Pavlovian.

The tour and the tales continue into the night and eventually Campo finds a nest to crash in. Where that was, he was not so sure. And then one night just simply rolls into another. A night on a bus, a night in a house, and often a sleep on a large cushion on top of a filing cabinet in what was glamorously known as the boy's trailer. Late summer quickly turns to autumn and before long and they are out wooding for fuel. Campo calls it home, for now. But he knows it won't last for long. Come the spring and their section 6, albeit faded and worn, is now replaced by the marching orders. The takeover and sterilising begins.

They all loosely agreed to resist. They knew it would be controversial for some, yet, for others there was not even a question. For many, this was almost a way of life now albeit reluctantly. Laws now so stringent and increasingly effective, evictions commonplace – and occurring with relentless regularity. For some this was an ideological struggle, for others an underclass war; and for the ever rampant development machine, this was just more dirt to be swept under the carpet.

Number 6 had been a bastion, a shelter, a history. From the Irish to the Brazilians, to the hippies and then the punks, these walls seeped stories. The gents were not to get their vacant genericification as easily as that. The occupants now barricaded in their sleep, as routinely as going to the shop.

Tables are nailed to windows; once front rooms - now naked and dark. Hefty joists are angled against the temporary barricades, and then fixed into blocks on the floor. Chaotic architects perfecting their stance. Experience led to effective resistance but this one was forlorn. The front of the buildings were well secured, but the back-door gets neglected. They had been at it for so long now that they were tired, they were worn. The monoculturists were on the march, London town now cleaned to make way for more of the same grey.

Sofas, armchairs, a coffee table, and a tall lamp with a lime green and gold shade are neatly arranged in a lay-by opposite the house. A living room out on the street. Armed with surrealism, many residents dressed for the part, now sit drinking coffee and staring at their once home from the outside. The system was cherry picking. They knew if they attempted to come for the whole of the street — at this time — would have been a serious battle. Instead they opt for a skirmish. Yet it was not going to be easy to reclaim this small terrace of six. These houses held life, gave life, a generation passed; some had been born in there and had grown up here. A sad but inevitable truth was felt in these transient times.

 Neighbours and spectators take their place as the darkness rolls into the road. The crew were both in and on the roof. The front of the house now totally secure. The Robocops trundled into position; their recent adoption of full body armour obscured their faces and humanity. The tactical support groups had evolved from the notorious special patrols, their sinister attire a sign of the times. But they remain as onlookers, as they play out their strange legal game. It is the bailiffs who go in first. Elderly and uniformed, they resemble removal men more than employees of the law. Blue, thick cotton working men's suits, the baseball cap their only defining feature with SHERRIFF painted across it in large white letters.

Following the paperwork, now nailed to the front door, the bailiffs proceeds in their ritual. Loud hailers shout routines, empty deals are played out. No one believes in the process but rules are rules and they have to conform. Then come the ladders, followed by a clamber three stories up. Sledge hammers and battering rams strike the fortress from the ground; the shudders of the old London stock can be felt from the roof. Tiles are smashed from the lower parts of the roof to make enough room for the old men to squeeze through, and into the attic they go. Momentarily the bailiffs disappear, swallowed by the dull, grey slates. And then all of a sudden, below the occupant's feet, they pop up and come smashing their way through. A specialist tool for the job, a forked and triangulated crowbar prizes slates away violently. The thin black tiles skid off the edge of the roof — a pause — then moments later shatter onto the ground far below. A bailiff breaks his way through with a sledgehammer and appears midriff amidst the roof. This abrupt, comical appearance of the Sherriff makes them all laugh. He's like a character from Camberwick Green magically appearing from a little toy box, a head and torso at their feet.

Natty Padlock swiftly whips off the Sherriff's cap while Gobby Dave seizes the moment and snatches at the incumbent's weapon of choice. Before the old man has a chance to respond, his ridiculously emblazoned hat is perched on his sledgehammer and quickly tied to the chimney stack for all to see. Roars, laughter and chants erupt from the street.

The line of Robocops remains in place and static; at times it is hard to tell if anyone, or anything, is inside those suits.

The bailiff loses control and thuggishly and pathetically strikes out at anyone he can find. He batters his way through the slate tiles, finally pulling his legs through the hole and begins a chase across the ridge of the roof. It is a strange sight, this old man up here on the rooftops. He is possibly in his sixties, or perhaps prematurely aged by the grimness of his post. Both sides are long-time familiar with each other, having played this pantomime out over and over again. Why they send in a few old boys first, whilst all the youth and brawn are below, remains unanswered? But this is their method and so little of it makes sense; their performance and procedure, *only doing my job.*

But this is now personal and froth is in the Sheriff's mouth. He makes a dash for Natty Padlock, looking like parkie chasing a kid. However, this is fifty feet up above and more tiles slip to their demise and explode dramatically on the ground. Gobby Mark has unclipped the Sherriff's keys from his belt and has now attached them to his cap along with the sledgehammer on the chimney stack. All those down below can see the goings on while the now furious official is the last to catch on.

By now the commander of the cops has decided to intervene. He has shouted at the ground force to stop battering their rams. The chief rapidly ascends the ladder and clambers into the roof, soon followed by his dutiful left and right. He shouts effectively at the bailiff who responds obediently, now utterly subdued in the presence of his superior. The headmaster scolds the caretaker, the game has come to its end. The rooftop protestors look sadly on at the old man, why did they send him up? Even though he is a brute, they feel his sorrow. Just another bastard pawn swept up in this sanitisation.

All the uniformed men retreat.

Well that's that for the day, they think to themselves. Campo watches the men in black subside, but he knows they can't retire themselves yet; it wouldn't be as easy as that. He slithers through the earlier skirmished scene and retraces the steps of the officers. Peering from the eaves of the roof he looks straight down below on hi-vizs, hard hats, and lines of men in orange. Africans and some Eastern European, the lowest paid now stand guard – protecting the bounty for those anonymous owners, who are never anywhere to be seen. Campo and co resign themselves to a night on the tiles and retire to the relative comfort of an attic.

The remaining five houses are empty, some secure with barricading, a mere veneer, that has worked. The security guards have formed their cordon and prepare for a long night's boredom, as those on the roof go explore.

Campo finds an unexpected gap in the partition wall. It is well hidden but now exposed in this former squatter's attic; possibly a rat-run between the buildings from unknown histories, secret passageways from before. Through this he squeezes and finds an empty and identical attic on the other side. He drops through the hatch and gently thuds feet first back onto the flat of a floor. He knows its empty but he listens intently, just for a moment, to be entirely sure. His torchlight searches the now desolate room. Discarded items, random and forgotten. A broken suitcase, an old scarf, some trashy old novels, and magazines – all now abandoned. He has nothing else to do, it's a long night ahead, and so he sits and flicks through the books. An old A4 black and white photograph falls out of an encrusted Hayne's manual, for the Land Rover, he accounts. Campo's torch illuminates the picture as he slowly picks it up to examine. A silhouette of a long haired youth: donkey jacket, flares, and big boots stand on a ball and chain swinging from a crane. Campo recognizes this same street; an end terrace now long gone to make way for a yard big enough for a bus or two. Resistance circa '77. The history resonates in the room, albeit for not much longer.

Come the next morning and the bleary roof sitters are awoken by the familiar sound of battering. Monotonous thuds strike hopelessly at the boards across well-sealed windows, the glass now all gone. Thud – thud — and thud some more. Splinters from the front door are heard yet the ferocity from yesterday is now more subdued; mundane – as they strike once more. They hammer and they bang but they can't get in. And so they bash some more. All the occupiers can do is sit and watch, as they slowly begin to accept that it is the day.

 Come mid-morning and cops had been sighted entering the other end of the terrace. The black ants now file in columns through a gap they have found (or made) and it won't be long before the building swells with an inundation.

 No words, just eye contact between each other and quick gestures are enough for the roof-sitters to decide it is time to escape. They can hear the doors being smashed below as the forces gather closer; house-by-house they come. A rope had been set, by which the activists all now climb, one by one. Off into the trees at the back of the park, sheltered by their leaves, perfect cover – and they are gone.

Campo runs for open ground, still managing to go unnoticed. He can't resist witnessing the final scene and decides to hide in a nearby bush.

Bailiffs, cops and guards are now all aware the buildings have become unoccupied and the beating of the houses is ordered to stop. The peaked cap is followed by the clipboard and a few robots for protection. Campo can see their faces as they walk down the back-alley of the houses and now they clearly observe the backdoor hanging off its hinges.

They stand, stupid, as they stare. This was always the easy way in.

If You Go Down to the Woods Tonight...

"Hear this - there is a woodland, not far from the village, that is said to be thoroughly haunted." Charlie looks up as he reads out from a page. Scouse snorts cynicism and chortles.

Charlie flicks through the pages of the local booklet of ghost stories he found on the bar: a spectre of a pipe smoking gypsy woman; a highway man who hides in the trunk of a tree; a coach and horses that have been heard on cobbles, where there are none... and there is a bush - if danced around three times, the Devil himself is said to appear. These are some of the tales of the supposedly most haunted village in England.

Charlie peruses the bar of this 16th, possibly 15th century (if not even older) hostelry. Dented and worn oak beams, dripping candles and a few drinkers who still sup from pewter tankards; this place itself has its fair share of phantastical history.

"This wood they say, is known as Fright Wood," Charlie continues to read out, not Frith Wood as they had been led to believe. Scouse's bemusement turns to a frown as he considers the dark tales of the woods; the very woods that both he and

Charlie had lived in for these last few winter months. Scouse stands up and stretches his full six-foot-four inches and roars loud enough for the heads of the other drinkers to turn, as he defiantly declares: "I ain't afraid of no ghost!"

He throws the remaining half-pint back and fearlessly strides to the bar for another.

A bell is tolled, last orders declared, and ones for the road are had before the drinkers return to the darkness.

A new moon is out but too immature to offer any significant light. But the tracks that lead to Frith Wood are easy enough to follow and assist the men in finding their way back to the camp. However, having returned to this wood following a tight squeeze through a gap in the hawthorn and finding themselves now under the canopy of the forest - there is no light; none whatsoever. They don't have torches. Instead, with bravado and possibly boyishness, they proceed with a regular nightly ritual: unto the pitch-black track that leads into the dark heart of the wood.

Charlie is never too sure if the abundance of ale assists or hinders. What one loses in balance is trumped by boldness and intuition. The black track of night always adds a little excitement to the journey home.

The left hand is held loosely in front of the face, protecting the now redundant eyes. Any low hanging branches, especially a thorn, could easily lead to permanent darkness if you weren't careful enough. The right hand is equipped with a whip of hazel, or any convenient dead wood, and is utilised as a blind man's stick — albeit much more aggressively — beating back any innocent scrub. But the real weapon of choice is the foot. Sweeping semi-circles are performed every time any doubt of your course is encountered; standing on one leg as the other searches out the raised boundary of the track. This action occurs every now and then, sometimes when a bend is felt, sometimes when a bush is crashed into, or sometimes simply to just reassure as these tracks had been well-rehearsed over this last season or so and it is the only way home.

A tawny owl calls to its nearby mate in the complete obscurity. Without fail, it always makes the two men startle -

breaking the absolute silence of the night. It reminds them both of the ghost stories. As they progress, possibly thirty feet apart, low mocking ghoulish calls are let out in childish attempts to spook each other. Scouse suddenly roars out into the dark in a thicker than usual accent, "Come 'ere while I batter you!" He defiantly challenges any phantasmagorical entities that may be lurking nearby. But none respond; not just yet.

Eventually base camp is found, defined by a final glow of an ember, before it calls it a night. The neighbours bid each other farewell and make final jests about ghosts as they part ways.

Standing alone for a moment, he listens to the fading crashes of his fellow drunk, heavily bashing his way through the undergrowth.

All becomes silent. Charlie shuffles to peer through the canopy to gain one last glimpse of the slither of moon that hangs in the clear, night sky. He is happy, content even, but the cold quickly gathers momentum, the moment the marching stops. His body temperature drops another degree as he reminds himself of haunted themes. Scared, yet not, he acknowledges the familiar vulnerability of the heart of this wood. All alone, Charlie embraces the isolation. He says goodnight to the ancestors, reminding himself of the essential nature of a constant fire; his now gone out. He shrugs as he throws back the hide of an Aberdeen Angus, which serves as a cabin door.

Charlie is immediately welcomed by warmth emitting from an old Aga stove. A faint glow from a crack in the steel does nothing to light the abode. He is routine and knows exactly where he left a candle - to be lit now.

The soft light illuminates the cabin, more of a shed to be honest. Four feet of panelled sides are topped by a series of bent coppice poles, some twined, some still holding their dead old leaf. Spider's webs occupy the gaps between the poles, sometimes sleepy wasps if you're unlucky. Random items are stashed for safe-keeping or simply to be easily found: newspaper; a corkscrew on a string; a book and a knife, are all deposited around the ribs of the cabin roof. A deep green tarpaulin tightly covers it all.

The shelter as a whole is squeezed tight between birches and hazel. Even in broad daylight it can only be seen from a few yards away; but then that is the point. The woodland expertly snuggles the camp, offering protection in the strongest of weather. During high winds there is little movement of the cabin, except for the occasional brush of bough tips that scrape slowly to and fro across the roof, like a tide. Now and then, quite rarely really, there can be a sudden draught; even during the stillest of times. It comes from below and billows the structure, briefly - like a sail. And this happens now.

It shivers through Charlie; someone has walked across his grave and now he has to work hard to avoid ghost stories sinking into his soul, before he embarks on his overdue sleep.

He is bothered, just a little shaken, you might say. He switches on his old radio set to break the silence and accompany him into this dark night:

Lehman Brothers have declared bankruptcy. Global stock markets are in turmoil, shares are falling dramatically. Merrill Lynch, AIG, Freddie Mac, Fannie Mae, HBOS, Royal Bank of Scotland, Bradford & Bingley, Fortis, Hypo and Alliance & Leicester are all in serious trouble.

Charlie is introduced to the outside dimension by this link to the World Service. It is a rare glimpse, this window, into the other world. Out here in the woods you can best ignore it all. Life is off-grid, off-radar, you are amongst nature, working through the days, coppicing, fencing, growing. Rarely other humans; just the occasional visit to the village for supplies and sometimes fuel and of course, an ale or two. Yet the belly of the beast is unbelievably close, just a few hours away. And here, now - the radio brings it into the cabin:

The neoliberal economic orthodoxy, which for thirty years has dominated the world markets, is suffering a major cardiac arrest of epic proportions. We have not seen anything like this since 1929. Western leaders have been assured of the resilience of their economic policies, yet now they are having to commit trillions of dollars to prop up the World Bank system; from here John it looks like the whole system could be in freefall.

It all sinks in as Charlie bends in search of kindling to restock his stove. Small sticks snap as apocalyptic images fill his mind. *Is it really all going to fall apart? Is this it?* In many ways it would be no surprise to Charlie. After all, this is what they had predicted, or dare say *felt,* for some years now. It was inevitable. The hyper-capitalistic hegemony had long been carried away by itself. The gamblers in the casino had been getting overly possessed by the demon greed, the unsustainability of the neoliberal agenda, the corporatisation of Western democracy, and the ignored ecological and human crises. *This is it!* The house of cards is tumbling.

Mortgage defaults are rapidly starting to rise, the national economy of the US is alarmingly beginning to falter, and overall John, I can definitely say - fear has decidedly crept into the credit markets. Lenders have now begun to seriously dread that their borrowers can no longer repay their loans.

Out here in the woods, would they notice the collapse? Plumes of smoke may rise from afar, distant gunshots perhaps, an abundance of sirens, and helicopter activity in the sky – maybe?

Charlie kneels and gently puffs on embers to encourage the kindling into fire. How long before they found them? Would it be instant martial law or simply a slower decline, as the panic sets in?

Charlie shivers at the news but glows as — phwoof! —his sticks take on the fire suddenly; he can now relax in the knowledge that his stove will warm him for the rest of the night. He knows he is going to have to stay awake for another half an hour or so to ensure that the fire has properly taken. His last task of the evening, is to emplace that final back-log for the duration of the night. To not do so would ensure a rude awakening with a frost on the inside of the cabin, and he didn't want that, ever.

Charlie now takes to his raised bunk and lies on his back, hands folded behind his head. He kicks off his boots from his feet, then kicks them again - off the end of his bed. He stares at the tarpaulin above his head, lost in the patterns of the cobwebs as he contemplates the collapse of civilisation – once again.

Tens of billions of dollars are being wiped off the international markets as the irresponsibility of some of these major players is now coming to light. It looks like the taxpayer is going to have to bail out the banks, John, and as it stands, we are still not sure if even this will be enough at this stage. Thanks David, it sounds like turbulent times ahead...

Charlie jumps up and snaps off the radio with intent. He has seen it coming for years, it stinks. His gut churns with anger. The fools. The bastards. He swears into the darkness, out into the woods. How could they? How did they let it go so far?

The silence of the woodland returns, except for the now roaring fire; it crackles and spits as drawn air joins the flames and eagerly rushes up and then out through the stack pipe. It is a still night and no other sounds come from outside. He is simply isolated.

Experiencing the solitude once again he ponders a walk into the village first thing the next morning. He envisions looted shops, burnt houses and chaos all around. Still not quite believing it is really happening, he shrugs, as there is nothing he can really do.

A couple more logs are now loaded into the stove and Charlie retrieves his book from the roof. Clambering back up to the bunk, then repositioning the candle, he finally lies back down to read.

The brown current ran swiftly out of the heart of darkness, bearing us down towards the sea with twice the speed of our upward progress; and Kurtz's life was running swiftly, too, ebbing,

ebbing out of his heart into the sea of inexorable time... I saw the time approaching when I would be left alone of the party of 'unsound method'.

Charlie hears a rat and thinks of bankers. He raises the staff he has for this task and pounds the floor of the cabin. It will see off the rodent for a while.

The word 'ivory' rang in the air, was whispered, was sighed. You would think they were praying to it. A taint of imbecile rapacity blew through it all, like a whiff from some corpse. By Jove! I've never seen anything so unreal in my life. And outside, the silent wilderness surrounding this cleared speck on the earth struck me as something great and invincible, like evil or truth, waiting patiently for the passing away of this fantastic invasion.

Charlie struggles to concentrate, his head full of rage. The gold, the ivory, the diamonds – nothing much has changed; it has now just run its course. This is it, this is the end; my friend.

Finally the back-log is snuggly fitted into the chamber of the stove. This ample chunk of oak was carefully chosen, just the right size, for this long and exceedingly cold night. A shovel full of fire-ash is carefully lowered onto the log and the draw shut down to starve the fire of any possible air. This will keep the stove in as long as can be; it should still be toasty on waking the next day.

Charlie still can't believe it, is it all really going to fall? They have their pigs, the goats and the vegetable patch. The water is not too far away. But of course, they will not be the only hungry ones. They are not armed, maybe they should have been? Who knows what it will be like, even if it is this time? If not, no doubt it will be soon. But what would it really be like? A sudden decline – total or partial, he still can't decide?

Prognostication continues... only three meals from chaos, the populous would erupt; would the military round them all up? *Who knows*! Would he be left alone in the woods, unseen? For how long? Days, weeks, months? Forever?

But his soul was mad. Being alone in the wilderness, it had looked within itself and, by heavens I tell you, it had gone mad.

A little owl lets out its eerie screech and breaks the silent night. Jack Frost goes to work as the cabin billows mysteriously once more; unnerving Charlie even further.

His mind is wracked and a twisted and unwelcome sobriety descends. He jumps off his bed, ruffles his hair, and rubs his face as if scrubbing.

The horror! The horror!

He searches for a jar and finds the right herbs dried from the summer past. He finds the cast-iron kettle and pushes himself just enough out through the door but he soon shivers in the night's crisp air. On opening the butt, its water has begun to freeze, so Charlie gives it a shake and a stir. Slushy iced water soon fills the kettle and a quick retreat is made for the fire. A poker is found and the plate of the stove lifts off. An imp-like flame tries to escape but is quickly squashed by the heavy, sooted and now full kettle.

The herbs go into a teapot and he begins a search for emergency spirts. The bottle is well stashed away from his neighbour, saved for such an occasion, should it occur.

Reluctantly he reopens the draw to the stove; it's going to be a long night he knows, as the night's air meets the fire – once again.

A gentle flutter joins the sounds of the stove, as Charlie looks around him. His eyes become fixed on a lone moth, obsessed with the candle's flame. He stares at it and follows it as it circles the candle for the very last time. Without moving, locked, Charlie gazes at the small winged thing, the colour of the forest itself. It is making its final flight. And now, as it snubs out its life - it kills the light in the cabin.

The darkness is complete.

Just Us

The alarm goes off. An arm appears from under a duvet. The small digital clock with its irritating tone is extinguished.

The transformation for Juno now has to rapidly begin. The Monday morning paradox commences, from dirty squatter to squeaky clean state operative. It is never easy.

Crawling along on auto-pilot Juno makes it into the becrusted cubicle. The less than powerful shower manages to penetrate some of his senses, enough to remind him of the weekend and produce a shudder for the day ahead. Bathing and hygiene have never been a highlight of the squatting life. But right now it is essential that all the evidence of a weekend's raving is scrubbed away — thoroughly — from the man who is about to re-enter the system, once again.

A crisp, white shirt is retrieved from a hanger, alien to this environment. A six-inch-nail, previously hammered straight into the bedroom wall, acts as a clothes rail. The now clean and dry Juno slides into his weekday attire and stands before the mirror. A

Crass poster, the one with the Sex Pistols (where their heads have been exchanged for the Queen and the Pope), stares out next to Juno's tie – which is grabbed in a hurry. Juno's eyes manage to peel open to reflect upon himself as he struggles with the knot. A cracked mirror, aligned by astigmatism, randomly decorated for no particular reason with stickers of gigs and demos, alludes to the renovation of this young man.

There is still techno in his veins; that sound of concrete in a tumble drier still persistent in his ears. His mouth is foul, as the weekend's residues still fail to subside. Looking himself in the eye he recalls the Saturday night. Euston, Central London and a botched attempt at a rave. They had managed to get the sound system into the basement of a long-time derelict building but the cops were so rapid and so intense, they all realised this time they had hit a main nerve. For a few hours a dozen or so crew were locked down underground as the force stood between the entrance and a few hundred, possibly a thousand party-people. Yet the law would not enter or intervene with the system below. As always, rumours and speculation quickly spread. Indeed, it was an unusual and unfamiliar stance from the Babylon. Some say this plain and anonymous building had turned out to be one of the state's very own - some say it is secret, some say the bunker is nuclear proof and an escape for the elite; stories abound. Word is out that the cops won't enter the building because — according to official secrets — this basement does not actually exist.

There is a surge in the crowd. Juno is right at the front and somehow has managed to get turned about-face in the melee with his back to the row of vigilant cops. And in that slow motion moment he catches sight of the latest toys of the state: the snatch squad and the video recognition team. A ball of men in black cling to a cameraman at the centre of their Romanesque huddle. This innocuous yet sinister device begins to scan the crowd. And all of sudden Juno feels the hook catch the fish, as he turns to his side and realises the scanner has locked onto Lee's face... and before he knows it, an avalanche of coppers breaks through the crowd; rabid.

There is no sound in his ears, no words in his mouth, as he realises, quite quickly what is going on. Juno makes a grab for Lee, an activist, a familiar - someone worth defending. But it's too late.

Lee is the last to notice as the snatch squad descends and deftly plucks him from the crowd. It is all over in seconds and Lee has gone.

Back in the room and Juno splashes his face with crap aftershave, his final attempt to cover the scent of this chameleon. Shoving toast and coffee into his mouth whilst grabbing his jacket, keys and phone, he pieces together the other party that he had managed to find at the weekend. There was always a plan B, but as usual it is all a blur, as he runs out of the door.

Down into the tube and re-emerging in the Elephant and Castle, the young squatter turned clerk, trots up the Newington Causeway. Just in time, he finally rushes towards the metal detectors and security guards at the entrance of the Inner London Crown Court.

Monday

Now seated at the feet of where the judge will sit, alongside his cronies and next to the witness stand, Juno takes his place in the old stenographer's chair. In front of him he checks his twin tape deck, sharpens his pencil and patiently waits for the beginning of this morning's trial.

All rise. The tedium of swearing in a jury commences. The judge emptily plays out his repetitive role. The game begins.

By and by a sorrowful Dutch truck driver is led into the dock. The Crown prosecution shares around photographs and jurors all leer towards exhibit A, B and C. Dustbin liners, all allegedly filled with ecstasy tablets at the time of this man's arrest. Unfortunately for the driver, the sacks were in the back of his lorry.

Juno is so close to the accused he can see the whites of his fingertips, all the blood presumably directed to his over-worked heart. The Dutch man gripped by fear watches over the court as his fate is determined. That is an awful lot of pills to be caught with.

Another pawn in the drug war? An evil, criminal mastermind waging terror on the souls on the English youth? Probably a too lackadaisical proletariat who has failed to check his load properly before entering the port, or one that has simply been duped. It is ironic to think what these three bin-bags represent. *There must be millions of pills being consumed each weekend*, Juno thinks to himself. Whole terraces of football fans spent their Saturday afternoon playing with huge inflatables, rather than the usual - killing each other for fun. Parties in every major city, numerous fields full of ravers. This was the nation's drug of choice right now. Rumours were spreading that the drinks company didn't like it because their customers were turning away from their national number one drug. It was all a farce, but it maintained the self-importance of the occupants of the courtroom, all except for the truck driver, of course.

The initial interest in the case for Juno soon wains as he goes about his role. Reading numbers off the cassette machine, writing the direction of the flow: Prosecution to defence; defence to the accused; prosecution cross-examination; judge to jurors... all recorded and their times written down.

The morning begins to pass slower and slower as the case unravels: the defence pressurising the inept prosecution, the prosecution defending back; the trial and the tribulation. And so it goes on...

Eventually they break for lunch. Juno reminds himself of the perks of this lowly paid post - the hours are short. Court always starts late and finishes early and regularly calls it a day.

But this afternoon's session involves a return to a different court room and a familiar, long running case. Juno rarely gets to see beginnings or ends of such cases. His role is just not that important, just a cog in their machine. But in this case of fraud, no one ever seems to be able to keep up and it appears to have been going on for over a year, possibly more.

Reams and reams of paper print-outs fill the desks of various clerks. Prosecutors and defenders all scrabble to find the place where they left off so they can resume their trial. It seems so easy to catch a dope with a blim, slap his wrist, bang him up, screw-up his life - after a quick case. But for a fraudster of the highest degree, a paperwork terrorist playing the game, possibly defrauding millions; these millions will be lost amongst more millions and all is far from clear. Bureaucratic banksters, with the same accent as the judge, they clear their way by deception, or is it boredom? Investigators never seemingly able to find that needle in the proverbial haystack. All their crimes obscured amongst these digits, those six-foot-high stacks of accounts. And so it goes on...

Tuesday

A last minute plan and Juno has had to change direction following a text to his phone from his faceless boss: Southwark Crown Court please. It is a long trip right across town but it's OK though, the trial won't start until eleven.

He takes his place, removes his jacket and sharpens his pencil for the day. What will it be? Larceny, corruption, an assault or another defraud... no, his guess is its drugs again as he watches two elderly Jamaicans being uncuffed, to take the stand.

The tall, black to grey dreadlocked men stand proud as the room starts to decide their fate. Their heinous crime, it unfolds, is to attempt to bring home some weed. Their cunning plan had been foiled as their humble stash was retrieved. Their methodology curious and somewhat amusing; not to just Juno, as he attempts to hide his smirk - better though than some of the jurors. These villainous pensioners had insulted the British justice system to the extent that they required an elaborate case by the Crown. Their dastardly plan was to bring ganja stashed in marrows from Jamaica, and this time they had failed.

Juno looks up at the women and men in their medieval wigs and gowns, as caped aristocrats deliver pomp and judgement upon these Rasta men. Highfalutin language separates the classes, but everyone really knows what is going on. These highest paid actors perform their daily role as players at The Globe. Under article this and according to that act, Jones versus Jones and the antiquated Misuse of Drugs Act of 1971... and so Shakespeare plays on.

The Rastas offer quotes from the Bible as their defence and a brief discussion of religious belief ensues, but Juno knows it won't last long.

Judge Dread is bored, and this, all can see. He has had enough and calls it time for tea.

A lukewarm substitute for coffee is filled into a small, brown plastic cup as Juno spends half his break in a queue. At least he has time for a fag. Retrieving his coffee from the machine he then enters the familiar smoking hole of Southwark's Crown Court.

It should be enough to put anyone of their bad habitats, this foul nicotine room. With its grey fag-burnt carpet, its yellowing walls and overflowing, communal ashtrays - the only furniture in this box. Quite often these rooms are entirely filled with tension. Defendants, witnesses, the accused and the abused all gather here to smoke their cigarettes down to the butt at such speed that their fingers burn. The room is usually full of a burgeoning underclass, all JD sports bags and white trainers under cheap suits. Occasionally one from another class enters, but only to retrieve a client for a brief. But today's group, to Juno's pleasure, is an entertaining one. Two tall women and a short man all smoke long cigarettes. Thigh high boots, tight, short skirts and revealing blouses, is not the normal attire for around here. The man wears an outdated and naff suit. Their conversation is not hidden and blurts out loud to a fourth party.

"They caught us red-handed." Details the taller of the two bleach-blondes. "I was spread eagle at the time, legs wide apart, flat on my back on the bonnet of a Porsche." She continues to titillate the room with their tale of how down in a Heathrow carpark — broad daylight she assures — they were in the middle of a porno shoot, when a security guard had stopped them short. "They usually like to watch!" She laughs. But not this time. Their voyeuristic speciality art had been interrupted by a job's worth, *Coitus interruptus,* I suppose you could say. She continues, at length, to give detail, which briefly made Juno's day.

A tannoy announcement interrupts them and Juno reluctantly stubs out his cigarette and returns back to the trial.

The Crown now brings forth its evidence, which, as it turns out, shocks the courtroom but maybe not as one would suspect. The only exhibits today, A and B, are the Jamaican marrows - from which the stash was retrieved. The clerk holds aloft two A3 sized sealed bags, their contents now two or three months old. The putrid and rotten vegetables swell menacingly, all liquid slime and grey-green, at the bottom of the bags. The judge is not amused but some members of the jury are. Ridiculous, contemptuous, put the bloody things away. The judge orders the packages to be removed from the court immediately, the colour of the CPS, now begins to fade.

Juno suspects Judge So-and-so has a game of golf later today, or maybe some other illicit engagement, that momentarily tantalises the imagination of this otherwise bored court employee.

Case dismissed. Technical complications, legal jargons and some spin for the jurors, whom have had a day out with a difference. All happy to have played their part. However, Juno knows the court is embarrassed by their own farce, the evidence wouldn't pass, the paper work wasn't in order and the elderly gents get to party once again. For this Juno is moderately relieved and that, for him, is now the end of his working day. This part of the job he likes, when he can go home at noon for a day's pay.

Juno squeezes into the train and meditates exhaustedly. He cannot wait to be home. Overland and then the tube, he counts his twenty two stops before he is back in his zone. Battery farmed commuters disgruntledly come and go. Juno is just grateful he does not have to do this long one every day. Eventually his stop at Kennington arrives and he finally arrives home.

Out of his suit and into his slacks and his wheeling and dealing resumes. He thinks of the judges and the barristers of this morning, as he folds another fifty into his wedge. All got to earn an honest crust, eh guvnor? He smiles to himself, if only they knew!

The room laughs at his stories, some almost finding it hard to believe, as they are so out of their realm. Others, more ardent, uncomfortable with this double-agent in the squat. Juno continually reassures them there is no plot. Just simply one day he had picked up his friend's phone who was not able to go to work and quickly dressed for the occasion and took his seat - and his wages at the end of the week, all amicably – of course! He has never met the boss, no interview, no CV – and more incredibly no criminal check. And this is where the excitement fills Juno. Only months before climbing cranes and taunting bailiffs and cops on actions, demonstrations - too many to mention here. Years of defiance, tipping the well balanced status quo, always trying other ways. And now he waltzes the innards of this beast's belly.

Security codes, trust, no apparent suspicion at all. Ultimately it is a perversion, some self-satisfying pursuit, just because he simply can. It is a strange game he is playing, but that's what keeps him going – and the £50 a day on top. He could plant a bomb in their chambers or cause some major disruption, but that's not his thing, which is where he meets disapproval from some black-bloc in the room. "I'm non-violent man!" He proclaims. "But surely there is something you can do to fuck things up?" An Italian all-in-black insists. But Juno just smiles and is happy with his insight, something he may be able to use at a later date.

Wednesday

Looking at his phone, somewhat thick from the night before, he sobers quickly after realising he has been summoned to the manor house: The Middlesex Guildhall. Address - Parliament Square. He shudders, he is now this deep in and that's for sure. It is a long road and no turning back. But Juno smiles to himself as he confidently readjusts his tie and steps out for the challenge of the day.

Amidst the penguins, clanking folded umbrellas as if ivory canes, Juno commutes with the upper classes into this heart of darkness - Westminster. All stone cut and iron railed, he proceeds to the far corner of Parliament square, away from the Commons, the Lords, and Big Ben.

Staring up at the grand expanse of the guildhall, always unconsciously looking for ways to climb, he smiles to himself as he brushes himself down for the last time. The Portland stone and the elaboration can deceive the age of such a building, art nouveau gothic they claim, Gotham City more like.

The security is most intense, yet from their manner and dress you would think that this was The Ritz. Juno stands star-shaped as a metal detector tickles his inner thigh. He saucily winks at the guard who sternly stares back with no smile. And off to court room three to see what sort of the day he will have.

He steps into the grandeur for his first time. Obviously overwhelmed and suddenly small fry, a kindly usher takes Juno gently by the arm and directs him to his place. As Juno sits he realises his nervousness and swallows a little too hard. A chemical sweat passes over him as debauched memories of the weekend flow past. He summons the depth of his will to hold steady and eventually they pass. Gulping from the bottle of water he then wipes the drips from his chin. The spectacle is immense, a cathedral more like. Five-foot blocks of stone, buttresses and eaves, a whole forest's worth of oak. It takes an empire to build such places as these. Gold gilded frames hold portraits of overseeing Victorians past. The court room at this moment is only occupied by the backstage crew, the ushers, and the clerks. But even they are caped and resemble extras from a historical film set or play. The Crucible, the 1957 version, Juno decides.

Barristers, lawyers and understudies carrying the full weight of the law; all now begin to file into court. Mutterings, whispers, but some so haughty they can be easily heard.

All rise for the judge - as wooden chairs scrape on wooden floors and echo around the chamber. Heads bow to God and to the Queen; but not Juno, he's still punk, but his reluctance goes unnoticed as all else have their eyes closed or are looking at the floor. Then the proceedings begin.

There is legal argument first, before a jury is sworn in. The language is exceptionally flowery today, code-like in its pretence. Making out most of what is said, Juno listens intently, but as with a part-learnt foreign language, he can only make out four-fifths. And then his attention begins to rise further. Covert operations, new laws made for surveillance by the police. Video cameras, facial recognition and new technologies not yet publically known to exist – all are presented with new jargon in this brief. This is followed by accented and heavily weighted words such as: activists, known-troublemakers, terrorist laws and the IRA. *What the fuck is this?* Juno freaks to himself as the monologue proceeds. Wanstonia, Hyde Park, the M11 and Reclaim the Streets. This is Juno's territory, all too familiar, the fear continues to creep. *Anarchist!* And the caped ones yaffle under their wigs. Whatever is going on, it seems the CPS have done a good job of convincing the court even before the trial begins. Innocent until proven guilty; but the judge will judge by appearances, especially after this speech.

The members of the jury are sworn in. It begins and Juno looks up as the public gallery starts to fill. Then the star of the show is led to the dock in his cuffs. It is Lee. Juno jitters and grinds his teeth, he is most unclear as to what is going on.

From that Saturday night snatch squad, now Lee is here delivered. His posture suggests he has taken a few digs on the way, the usual gift from the pigs although their professionalism has extended to managing to avoid any bruising to the face. The mild-mannered Lee, looks drab and understated, but the court treats him as a wild beast. The public gallery swells to fifty or more; Juno and they begin to recognise each other one-by-one. And then Lee looks over to Juno. Both are well-rehearsed in matters such as these: emotions exploding, but animation restrained. Looks of bewilderment and mistrust are all now directed at Juno. Some say later they thought that Juno was gonna spring up and handcuff himself to the judge as a protest. Others suspected he was an undercover. But this was no time for surprises, Juno now sits in a very hot seat. And as the show begins with Lee's charges being read out, the gallery erupts in jeers and hoots. The judge quickly responds. The hammer slams over and over and he gets to play his favourite part: *Order, order...* then silence and they start.

Essentially it is an assemblage of minor offences, day-to-day stuff of an activist: broken bail conditions; broken locks and bolt-croppers; obstructing an officer; obstructing a highway; a breach of the peace – trespass and so on. But it's not looking good for Lee as the use of language inflames the court: threats to the state; lawlessness; deviant public enemies and the over abused word - terrorist. Lee looks as if he has already been condemned to hang. His narrowed shoulders could not slump any lower. But then the defence takes his turn: articulate, well-educated but also well-read and obviously sits on the other side of the fence. He bombards his opposition and delivers his heartfelt response: Freedom of speech; freedom of expression; environmental destruction and the importance to democracy of diverse and alternative beliefs. The wigs mutter unconvincingly amongst themselves.

Then the first police officer steps up to the stand. Hand held on the Bible, he swears to God with the same sincerity as if the almighty had fallen down the stairs himself. He rolls a little of his sleeves up, fingers his collar and flips open his notebook. Wetting his thumb he finds his place and begins to read. Struggling with the longer words, as with marbles in his mouth, the young officer orates his version of events. Then the duty doctor makes his appearance. He searches his memory from his day to day stuff. He looks overworked, sketchy and under pressure. The doctor goes on to defend the police methods of restraint, as the cross-examination delivers numerous photographs of bruises and hand marks around Lee's torso and neck.

Then cop two and cop three try and keep their stories straight. Amongst their monologues and the monotony, Juno has been alert to mistakes. Evidently, so has the defending lawyer. He has heard the inconsistencies and he subtly looks over to Juno to check if he is paying attention and getting this all down. Juno avidly writes notes in his log. The clarity of the defence rips through the not-so-bright officers of the law. They had looked like they were doing so well. The tennis continues as lies and counter lies are volleyed across the court. Why are the bruises and the neck marks from twelve hours after the arrest? Why was no food or water given for his duration in the holding cell? What are these inconsistencies in your reports? It is suddenly the Met who are on trial. The defence is on fire but quelled by the prosecution. *Objection your honour,* he intercedes. *This is slanderous, your honour,* he pleads. His interruptions are shallow and all overruled, however, they are disruptive and possibly enough to confuse the court, especially the amateurs amongst the jury.

Finally the judge calls lunch. The case is 50/50 and could go either way. The court rises, waits for the judge to leave, and all disembark except for two.

"Can I order you a sandwich?" The advancing defence calls out to Juno, as he shuffles papers on his desk. A bewildered Juno looks up and without words communicates - *what do you mean?* The lawyer explains they have work to do and there will be no lunch break today. This is an anomaly for Juno, but he knows exactly what he means. They both smile at each other, comrades now, so the co-conspirers get to work.

"Yes, here it is, I have marked it down." Cop 1 at 11:23, the next at 114:012.

"Yes I have the contradictions," Juno confirms.

The barrister replies, "Good man!"

A junior appears with lunch. Sandwiches and drinks above the standard of Juno's normal expectations. He takes a bite as he rewinds, fast forwards and finds the right place on the tape. Listening intently to the tiny sound coming from the machine, the monotones come out clear.

"Yes, there you go!" The lawyer claims. That should be enough evidence for a wrongful arrest, they have foolishly said as much themselves. Juno fast forwards some more. "Aha! Here we are again." The character impersonates one of Conan Doyle's, yet is unaware that he does. The duty doctor's time of examination do not match the time since arrest and their attempts to hide their black and blue justice is thwarted. "Go on, go on... there is more to be had."

Juno has no affection for lawyers, intensified since his time in this post. The irony of these members, some of the highest paid in the land yet they are some of the biggest scoundrels in these courts. Charlatans, leeches, some of the grandest liars of all. These Bullingdon boys, at the top of their game, show contempt with their every breath. Hundreds of pounds per hour to prance about in fancy dress. Yes there is the odd good one, with justice truly in their hearts, but the rest are savagely intent on keeping the money in their centuries old families, at a high cost to everyone else. But this lawyer who stands before Juno right now, is unusual, a one in ten (probably a hundred.) He is not from the same class; this is someone who must have trudged that extra mile, fought harder than the rest, and genuinely earnt his place in this league. He has an agenda and strong held beliefs, this would not be obvious to all, but from where Juno sits he can sense the barrister's mission easily.

And sure enough between the two of them they break the case in their lunch break and have it all wrapped up before the first of the attendants reappear.

It is all over before the jury are in or the public gallery is re-opened. The now seemingly private case with just the essential players in the room. The tapes are played back, the points raised. There are times of silent intensity, except for the odd groan. The prosecution appeals once or twice but soon fades into hopelessness, as it is clear to all of the room— the cops have spectacularly cocked it up — once again.

Lee is brought forward and his expression does an about turn. He thanks his luck - but holds bitterness for his own injustice, which he knows will be impossible to attest; the double-edged sword of this game. He would be a fool at this stage to pursue the assault, the wrongful arrest and so on. So he knows, once again, as with the law – they all make their own rules once back out on the street.

Thursday

Running a little late, Juno makes it to court room three of the Inner London Crown Court. He looks around the room as he gathers his papers and himself. It is unusually busy with what he realises are technicians frenetic about the place. They are fixing TV screens around the courtroom. Two screens either end of the jury box and two standing apart on stands in front of the bar and the remainder are being fixed, left and right, on the judge's bench. From where Juno sits he can see only the backs of the six screens.

Hmmm, what have we here today? The case begins and Juno quickly catches up with a vice raid from Soho, nearby. He can't quite follow the case, it must be quite some way in. But he is surprised to hear that the judge and the jury and all of this court are to spend their morning watching extreme porn. Apparently they have to decide if it is offensive. Surely this is a matter for boards of censors, not jurors, but the Judge has deemed that this is part of the evidence of an on-going and complex case.

The level of red faces is immense. The very British way of discussing sex is hilarious. The prudes and the hypocrites are all in the mix, as barristers now have to demonstrate the Crown and the law's views on such activities. Sadomasochism, felching and fist-fucking all have to be uncomfortably spelt out. The position of the law, you see, in matters such, is all there in the books. Like school teachers in that awkward sex education lesson, the lawyers have to detail lewd acts; which are obviously way past the imaginations of some of the very innocent looking jurors. The judge, however, appears to know exactly where it is all at.

And so the video begins.

The judge seems familiar, perhaps knows the film well, as he covers his grin with his hand. Juno has the oddest seat in the house. Not able to see one screen at all, only their backs. Just the faces of the immersed viewers and the sounds from the performance. It sounds like a really fucked up farmyard, all grunts, squeals and groans. The bench holds steady, their stiff upper lips well trained, but they look as if they are being tortured themselves, but will not confess. But some of the jurors, oh boy! Their faces. Juno slowly and carefully studies each one.

Middle-aged housewives, perhaps retired teachers or those that have spent their lives working in a bank. They have never seen anything like this in their innocent lives. Some are so shocked you would wonder as to their health. Necks irritated, all bright red as a rash, cheeks even redder and eyeballs swollen in their sockets. Some simply do not know which way to turn. Compelled by their duty, their novelty few days out, but no one ever expected this. Now trapped in the jury box, crammed in, all twelve. And the show goes on, and on and on... the judge is loving it, Juno can tell. But some of the most innocent jurors look they have just taken a daytrip to hell. Juno has to match sound effects to reactions, a game he is most enjoying, as he can't tell what is seen. Obviously a large and unreasonable insertion is taking an extra-long time, judged by the cries of pain. Some of the jury have hands to their faces, some simply can no longer look.

And so it goes on until the judge decides it's time for a nice cup of tea.

The rest of the morning remains intense with much discussion about the decisions that need to be made about those that may be have been under duress, underage or coerced. The amusement for Juno has now passed, not much left to snigger about, as the courtroom now feels like cleaners scrubbing a dungeon after a particularly excessive session. Juno's stomach rumbles as he thinks of his lunch. A lawyer continues to educate the jurors about various sex toys and some very specialist vices.

After his midday break spent outside on a bench and half an hour of some welcome sunshine, Juno briefly manages to clear his head. Watching the one-footed pigeons, the tourists and the suits; it all seems so normal out here, this far over-ground.

For the second half of his Thursday, the court recorder is summoned to court room number seven. The very last of the courtrooms, curious Juno thinks. It is upstairs, down the end of a very long corridor. On entrance it appears more like a long banquet hall than a court. Heavy felt curtains are drawn in places to keep out the now warm afternoon sun. Otherwise, various oak tables and benches are lit by strong shafts of light.

Again, as this is a case in afternoon session, Juno has no idea of the content of this trial, but instantly senses the collective unease in the room. It is intense, sombre and much pain can be felt. Juno looks over at the jurors with their clasped hands, heads bowed at the floor, as in prayer.

He is soon to pick up the pieces of abuse and assaults, as various young females take to the stand. The accused, a supposed gent, a practitioner, an osteopath or some sort of masseuse. The case is taken very seriously, this type of trial is in another class. Professional women stand in the dock, close enough for their perfumes to waft into Juno's face. Solicitors, accountants, and some secretaries all give brief, but similar accounts. Their spoken evidence overwhelming, the room can barely look up. The defendant is expensively besuited. He wears a gold and black masonic ring on his little finger, a familiar sight around here. But it does not look like the symbolic jewellery will be able to work its magic this time.

In cases such as these, the personal accounts are overwhelming, but the defence does its best to breakthrough. The afternoon versions of those affected by this man's acts is case closed as far as Juno is concerned. And, by the looks of it, it is the same conclusion for the rest of the room.

However, today they will not discover the outcome; the Judge calls time on the day's proceedings. The accused's defence statement will have to wait until the following day.

Juno decides to walk home, over London Bridge and south into his zone. The sun is out as he trundles along with the rest. His head and heart are heavy, despite this pleasant late summer's day. All that for just £50 and he reconsiders his position, after all, this is how it always turns out in the end. The disparity, the hierarchy and social division suck. Each day spent with selfgroomers who *really* believe they are doing a good job. But for Juno it is all upside down. It's all so feudal, a medieval institution, they are still trying to stop the peasants from poaching the laird's best game.

Juno sinks further into his contempt. Just another day at the office, dear – we can now all go home for our tea.

Friday

It has been a long week for Juno, some extraordinary cases for sure. He is now not so sure of the excitement, the usual drudgery may be welcome recompense. But for the meantime it is back to Parliament Square and over to the Middlesex Guildhall again, for the last day of the week.

A less than impressed Juno watches this morning's trial with greater contempt than usual. An African, a Senegalese to be precise. English his third maybe fourth language, but he can hardly speak up for himself. Stocky, broody, obviously not well. This tragic comedy begins to play itself out.

He is a bank robber, at this Juno is surprised. But he is not a successful one, obviously. The judge and some of the bench relish this and have saved up their favourite speeches as if it's Al Capone in the dock. The severity, the harshness, the importance that this man needs to know what a bad thing he has done. And then comes the punch line as the evidence for this great robbery is brought forth. This desperado has held up a bank, his weapon of a choice - a banana; I joke not. Order is brought to the court, the juries sworn not to laugh. This is not a stroke of genius, bringing in a concealed fruit through a metal detector into a bank, but an insane act. Juno can see, not just by the excessive sweat of the accused's brow, but his general misdemeanour spells illness, of the mental kind. There is a distinct lack of compassion in the court, it is all too obvious to see. The man is probably schizophrenic, he needs help not incarceration, as this is undoubtedly his fate. And so it goes on and the judge tells the man what a naughty boy he is and how a few years in the jail and a little word with the home office will sort him out. Juno simply shakes his head.

By the afternoon Juno is bereft of any humour, certainly it's been lost over this long week. He now sinks further as he gets the call to courtroom seven, once again.

He has missed this morning's defence statement from the health practitioner, although he cannot imagine what the accused has managed to say, in light of the evidence previously offered to the court. But what is this now? As Juno takes his place, another yet most unusual legal argument ensues. A P.I.I. is called.

Public interest immunity, it is all there in the name. Under the Crown Court rules (Criminal Procedure and Investigations Act 1996) (Disclosure) Rules 1997, for those that might not believe this. In effect it is the procedure that follows an application to the court for non-disclosure of material. And this is exactly what happens now – and the Judge nods just once in agreement to the request, as if he had just bought an expensive painting at an auction. The sweat now permeates the back of Juno's shirt as he knows what is coming next. A P.I.I., why here, why now? These are matters to be discussed in private, no knowledge allowed to the jury and are usually saved for such occasions as hiding the identity of grasses, IRA informers, that ilk. Sometimes they are used for other forms of intelligence or to protect journalists' sources in sensitive cases. But not today.

The jury are called back to the court and the Judge briefly explains to them the turn of events and then they trundle back out again for yet more tea. Next the judge addresses the bench and then the court recorder: they are to convene privately in his chambers, in ten minutes.

Juno has no time for anxiety and steps up to the mark, but he will have to be quick as he has to retrieve a hand-held tape recorder from the other side of the building. Quickly pressing codes, running labyrinths, slamming doors and Juno is there and back again and heads off down the now grandest of all the corridors, which leads the way to the judge's chamber.

He can hear them, he stops just around the corner, gathers himself and tries to regain his breath. Composure. Poker face. He wipes away a little sweat.

"Ah there you are," bellows the judge, now bald, no wig. The two lawyers are with him, their little white bows appearing even more ridiculous now they have disrobed. Both hold ribboned documents under their arms, as they all enter the judge's chamber. Juno is the last one in and is asked to close the door, the others are offered chairs but he is just a fly on the wall. He has got to get this right, technically at least. As he fiddles with his tape recorder and finds an appropriate place to stand. Not too close as to interfere, but he needs this on tape, although this will undoubtedly be the very sort of tape to soon get conveniently lost.

They proceed with their private hearing. The judge sits behind his desk; awards, trinkets, golden picture frames, facing him, but who knows what they may portray. Juno tries to relax by imaging the judge as a character from Harry Potter, but fails as the figure soon turns into Dr John Dee.

"Now see here, in regards to this case, I have a letter of the upmost importance, unusual, I am sure you are aware, but here it is and that's that." He unconvincingly reassures the two men of the bar. Juno looks around the antiquated room: 1930s? 1630s more like. And the judge unties and rolls out a gold edged scroll, breaking the red, wax seal at its base. He lightly discards the silk ribbon to one side, as he tilts his head back to read through his half-moon spectacles. One hand holds the scroll at the top, the other keeps it open at the bottom. The judge clears his throat and reads out in his most pompous tone yet.

It is a letter from the palace, yes *the* palace; from a Princess in fact. She is a regular client of the accused, a jolly good chap by all accounts. And that is pretty much that.

And so it goes on...

The Road to Oranmore

Twenty two hours later, or thereabouts, Danny eventually gets off the bus. It's a long way to Tipperary, even further to Galway; you will have to excuse the puns at this stage. Danny greets the sun with a stretch of relief and steps out with the same wobbly legs as he had on the ferry at dawn. It has just gone two o'clock in the afternoon. It's bright and blustery, in that familiar west coast way. He counts the change from his pocket. Danny has enough for a pint and a packet of fags - that will be the last of the money, so he might as well spend it in style.

He steps off the backstreet, just past Eyre Square, and into the familiar underwhelment of an afternoon bar. One man slumps as another checks his paper against the racing horses on a TV screen, which is perched up high in the far corner. A radio just about drowns out the sound of the sports commentator. A bar tender, drying a glass with a tea towel, looks up as Danny strolls in like it's the Wild West.

Young Danny takes a wooden stool at the wooden bar and orders a pint of stout. The tired traveller uses the time whilst his pint settles before the bartender returns to give it a head. Danny gets up and approaches a cigarette machine. He puts in his coins and a few fall out. He has mixed his denominations, some English change is rejected from the machine. This time he gets the money right and is rewarded with a wide, green and white packet of Majors and returns to the bar.

His now ready pint sits gallant on a beer mat. Momentarily admired. Then gracefully he sups with his eyes closed.

Walking down Madison plays on the radio. The lower windows of the bar are painted out with only the upper ones letting in light, half of them are stained glass. Through these coloured rays of light Danny contentedly blows smoke from his cigarette as if it were a Cuban cigar. He listens to the music as he folds under the top of his fag packet and smiles to himself.

From an uptown apartment to a knife on the "A" train
It's not that far
From the sharks in the penthouse to the rats in the basement
It's not that far

The song is in New York but it's not lost on Danny, he is in the opposite port – just the Atlantic apart. Kirsty MacColl's singing is movement and unfamiliar streets. It's his moment too, this is where Danny actually is, moving – again; at last.

Refreshed by his pint; topped up from the fill he had on the ferry first thing this morning, along with all those homecoming songs for the Irish. He takes one last look at the white suds that slide down the innards of his now empty pint glass, stands up and leaves the bar, unnoticed.

Its festival time and the summer is at its best for these parts. The streets are lined with bunting and an abundance of visitors and shoppers. He strolls towards the centre with his rucksack slung over one shoulder. Light in his step, slightly swaggered, Danny is still walking down Madison with Kirsty. He whistles along to the tune in his head and eagerly anticipates the months ahead.

On these cobbled and narrow back streets he comes across a crowd on a crossroad. Buskers — good ones — hold the attention of a surprisingly large group of onlookers. A penny-whistler sits on the floor cross-legged as a mandolin takes the lead and a bodhrán player thumps along perfectly (with a tipper made from a bone). It is the familiar sound of here. A barefoot, waist-coated, young type with cut-short trousers impresses all with a diablo. Danny has seen it all before but this particular performer holds his attention. He flings his diablo high-up above the crowd, spinning so fast it looks out of control. A bit risky Danny decides but looks on with a respectful smirk. To smash someone in the face with a missile at that speed would definitely be show-over and probably a run down the street. But this character has the bravado and the skill to land his craft on the bunting line ten-feet above the crowd. Whoops and jeers and hands clap, as the crowd watch the colourful spinning top as it follows the line of bunting across the street. A quick parting is made as the jester runs under the line to the other side of the road. He is just in time when the diablo begins to slow. As a tightrope walker loses their balance, the spinning device falls back down to earth, and is expertly caught on a cord between two sticks. Spun quickly, flicked a few more times for speed and effect, and the street performer tosses the spinning top high into the air once more. The crowd adore him; at any other time they probably wouldn't even look him in the eye.

Fair play, fair play – Danny joins in with the clapping and sidles his way over to the buskers, as the crowd now throws coins at the show. The musicians pack their things away while a few others linger with their dogs on strings. A woman, a small child and a Lurcher hound - all stand staring out to different bits of space. This is who Danny tentatively approaches. But they are friendly; the woman engages in some chit-chat, nice show and all that. Her accent distracts Danny, northern yet West Country, perhaps Welsh borders, he is not sure. Mary, her name turns out to be, is the wealth of information that Danny had sought. He is relieved to have found a source of news this quickly and is keen to join the others. However, the news is a mixed blessing - trouble with the law. Mary gives details of the previous days: the Gardaí blocking last year's camp, a few scenes out on the road. Some vehicles had managed to find a small camp to park up, but there was no grazing and a big group of horses have had to gather eight or nine miles down the road, maybe more, on the coast. This is not the news Danny had wanted, or expected, to hear. Neither is it a surprise, it's always like that, and so Danny musters another plan.

With no money, no taxi, and probably too long to walk before it gets dark, Danny takes up Mary's offer to go back to her site nearby and see what they can find.

It is squashed in wasteland, surprisingly close to town: a few trucks, a van, and large coach are parked in a line next to mounds of recently dumped spoil. The long, grey and white coach sits low on its suspension and has a cartoon painted near the front door - Roadrunner from the Looney Tunes. This was a very fast bus back in the day, Mary assures Danny with an ironic smile, as they enter through its double doors. The vehicle is packed; part session, part slumber. The calculations in Danny's mind are quick to deduce that there is nowhere to sleep here tonight.

Danny is introduced to the residents; all raise a drink. Some old faces, some new. Danny grabs a dirty old tea mug from the sideboard, gives it a quick rub with his shirt and gets given a shot of cider out of a scrunched plastic bottle. It's good to be in company, it's good to have a drink, but Danny's next observation is no one here is fit to drive. Pulling out a smoke and instantly blagged, Danny's packet of Majors gets passed round and less than half a packet are handed back. Danny ponders tagging onto this session, maybe a few drinks and a laugh all right, but it's obviously overcrowded and you'd be lucky if you got to kip down on a dog's blanket for the night. Danny looks back out the door at the broken concrete track, looks up at the gathering dark clouds in the sky and rules out sleeping outside. He has got to keep moving, so he brings the subject up. Sniggers and jeers and 'yer fooked man' are all they can offer. Danny begins to regret the turn of events. It's a shit road to hitchhike and deadly in the dark. But Mary has a plan and offers Danny one of the kids' bike, a red BMX. It will have to do.

And so our weary traveller accepts his position and without further ado adjusts his rucksack upon his back, which feels bigger than the bike, and pedals off…

There is no sitting down, the saddle feels like miles from his arse. There is only one speed, full speed; he just has to peddle fast. By and by, through the centre, the suburbs and the sprawl, he now takes the road west and then south out of the town. He joins the N18, all quiet except for one tractor, and crosses some bogs but its turning out to be much further than he thought. Into a drizzle he peddles furiously some more, his legs begin to protest. He eventually reaches the place they call Oranmore; there is not a soul in sight. He reluctantly accepts there is still a way to go to get to the bay, so he follows his nose towards the coast.

Thirsty and sweating heavily, he is relieved to find an old cast-iron pump at a spring beyond the edge of the town. Dismounting he throws his now heavier ruck-sack to the ground and briefly rubs his shoulders. He takes the serifed metal arm and begins to pump up some water. As the first drops appear he examines them in one hand. He temporarily stops pumping, pokes the water with his finger and looks closely at the remaining contents in his palm. A few specks, no sheen, he pumps harder and the water comes through good and clean. He fills one hand and sups enthusiastically, but soon surrenders to sticking his head under the flow, still just managing to extract the water with the pump handle in the other hand. Cooled and refreshed, he heads off once again.

Out onto the barren and bleak coastal back tracks that seem seldom used. He can sense the edge of the land, smell that not so far-off sea, but it is becoming unclear as to which way to go. A crossroads is reached, no sign posts at all and the same view in every direction with not a person to be seen. *Just give us a scent,* the young rider pleads to the sky. He dismounts, throws off the ruck-sack once more, followed by the bike onto a grassy verge. He stands very alone in the middle of the four roads, hands on hips. He has no time to get lost, soon it will be dark and a night in a field would be a wet one by the looks of the incoming clouds.

One road can be eliminated, hopefully, the one that's just been ridden down; so that leaves three. The sun slowly sinks behind murky mists, but it's out to the west, over the sea and offers little in the way of clues. Danny knows its all coast with many meanders and bays; to keep your bearings is not going to be easy around here. He walks a few minutes south, turns around and returns to where he started. He walks north, turns around and heads back to his original spot.

Go west young man, go west. And Danny spots his gold: horse-shit lying lumped in the middle of the fourth road. It's fresh as well. Danny now knows this is the way. He jubilantly continues on his quest. Yet doubt quickly seeps in, what if this is from a single horse? A local rider out for a jock. Then more manure, his doubt extends to possibly two horses that may have been ridden out. But then he sees one of the equine deposits has been flattened by cart wheels and he is suitably convinced he is on the right track. He picks up speed and cycles past more and more signs dropped on the road, like Hansel and Gretel's breadcrumbs, showing him the way home.

Eventually he reaches the top of a dirt track which drops down towards the bay. He can see smoke rising from the camp, with less than an hour or so of light left. What a day.

Standing for a moment, bike held between his wobbling legs, Danny takes in the scene in front of him. That's a lot of wagons — maybe twenty or more — parked in a semi-circle. All tucked away in a corner following the contours of a stone wall and the hedge line. The green tarpaulin covers upon colourful carriages of all shapes and sizes sets a remarkable sight. He recognises most, names them to himself, but not all. Amber shafts from the setting sun punch through the broody clouds and illuminate the camp with a gorgeous, soft evening light. There is a long, green peninsula that curls out into the sea and an inlet that has formed a small lake. There are horses, lots of them, too many to count right now. They are untethered and graze freely alongside goats and chickens in this self-contained camp; and of course the camp is full of people, dogs and kids. The spectacle is most impressive. Danny rubs his face, quickly recovers himself from his moment of sentimentality and boldly remounts once more.

The first of the dogs bark and soon gather into a fearsome pack. Danny offers his hand to the first few, the ones he knows from time. The hounds do their thing and all seem to agree that he is welcome so they let him through, except for an odd persistent one at the back that is now shouted at by someone nearby.

Faces look up from squatted positions around the fire: buckets, pans, suds and water – its clear-up time after dinner. Recognition dawns on the various faces and soon they all gather around Danny. There's some welcoming embraces from the women and big slaps on the back from the big men, who have now begun to appear in the camp. The slaps and the hugs get harder as the closer the family gets. It's a joyous reunion, but brief, as early evening tasks are to be tended, and all get back to their chores. Except now the hearty and round Mikey encourages Danny to follow him by the command of his waving hand and a tilted head gesture; he was never one for many words.

"There ya go." Mikey directs in his deep Athlone tone and throws back a cover off his four-wheeler cart.

"Tarp, enough poles – you might have to blag some string, and 'ere, look, an old can stove. Let's see if we can find youse a stack pipe."

"Nice one, bless ya." Danny gratefully replies, as Mikey leaves him to it.

Looking up at the sky, Danny already knows he better be quick and sets about looking for a pitch nearby.

He finds a good spot, just off the back of the circle and nicely tucked into the banked hedge. He now judges the prevailing wind, which is fair obvious as they are down on the coast, but he needs to get it right if he doesn't want to be woken in the night by any nasty surprises. Taking a hazel-pole in hand he now paces and mentally maps out his camp. Testing the ground by stabbing with the stick, *yes good enough*, he returns to the fire in search of some tools.

"A cup of tea." Eve holds one out, as if by magic, as Danny approaches the fire. "Timely." They smile at each other.

"I'll need a stake, a hammer and some string." Danny requests as all he has got is his Opinel knife.

As the light goes down and the night draws in, the tired traveller looks up above. Venus is the first to show herself in the evening sky. He looks back at his bender tent and thinks not bad, it will do. It's very basic, just the poles and the tarp, his ruck-sack now thrown in on the grass, but it is hardly home yet. Then Mikey re-appears with a fold of carpet and two deer skins that puts a smile on Danny's face. They fix the stove in, having borrowed some flexi-pipe, a bow-saw and sourced some half-decent firewood. Danny is modest, but knows their generosity will only last this night, until he sorts himself out. He knows the fine line between a welcome guest and burden, all too well.

The stove is primitive: thin, cut tin, with the paint burnt off. It is placed on a large stone that had been found in the hedge. But it draws a treat and dries off the eternal damp of the west coast, a greater necessity than providing heat at this time of year.

The wood burner is a bit of a death trap, soon glowing bright red. An unhealthy combination of sharp edges of metal for doors and a loose fitting stack-pipe, but it'll have to do for the night. The young lad rolls out his army surplus sleeping bag, feels snug, pulls over the front of his bender and goes straight to sleep.

The deep slumber ends amidst all of the early morning sounds: a bleating goat, a crying baby, a squeaking cockerel and a few already up and running kids. Danny can also make out the sound of coffee being ground. Stepping straight out into the dense early morning dew, the pressure so high the sky seems far away. It is a perfect morning – in every way.

Gathered around the fire-pit, sat on old metal trunks (the food boxes) and all are trying not to watch the kettle. The intimacy of the camp unfolds for the day. There is no greeting your neighbours after a shower and a spruce. Out here you all rise together, bed hair, bleary eyes – one and all.

Thick, black, hot coffee is poured into Danny's mug as others opt for Barry's Gold Blend Loose Leaf tea, with a splash of fresh goat's milk. The caffeine works instantly and our refreshed traveller begins to tell his tales. Not much news reaches these parts, with only a few passing through here and there. Big sites on European river beds and in La Linea too - the front line, he orates. Good parties in the Valley, all happening down in Andalucía and over the border, the dwellers around the lakes of Santa Clara have to get a mention too. His tales roll on, as more coffee is poured and details of England are what some are most keen to hear. Huge raves, reclaimed streets, and people living in the trees. He saves the worst for last as he knows this is what they want to hear. And each gets to relish their freedom and their choices on this bright and beautiful morning on the beach, about as far west as you can get. The terminal torydom, the criminal justice bill, and the braying morons of the British press – Danny purposefully and chronologically reads the news. All now appear appeased and relieved to be so far away from the rot.

Stories are exchanged and Danny gets to hear their news. It reads like the guest list for Noah's Ark. This baby born here, and that new baby over there, those puppies there and these kids here. And then this mare and that horse and these colts have been bred, the most amazing foals so far. This listings are extensive.

He takes in the scene; fertility all around. As nervy chicks peck around his feet, he looks up to the three recently-born babies around the fire and smiles. There are young animals and children everywhere, it is now summer - it must have been a helluva spring. Life pumps around the camp.

The thwack of a sliotar on a hurley stick resounds from just outside the camp. Two tall and lean Irish lads, Mullagh and Jimmy Mulligan, lob and hurl together. The ground now thuds as Mikey is joined by Red Brendon, both mounted high on their horses, one mare and one stallion, respectively. The hefty and hairy footed piebalds come closer to the fire. It's an incredible height especially when viewed from sitting down, to look up at the rider sat upon fifteen or more hands. They both ride bareback, tilted backwards, bollocks tucked up, reins held high – for a good look as much as anything else.

"Come on! Let's take 'em for a swim!" Hollers Mikey, as he leads his horse about face and turns away from the fire.

No time but this moment and all immediately get up and go.

One by one, riders gather on their finest. Excited animals call out to each other; neighs start to echo around the bay. A few stand tall on their stallions, others now appear on weighty and long-haired mares. Long flowing socks of white, coarse manes, some with big 'tashs: piebalds, skewbalds – a grand looking bunch.

"What ya got for me?" Yells out Danny, still on terra firma and in need of a horse.

Trivet Dave runs past, alongside his mare, John Wayne style... and leaps, mounts and shouts to Danny,

"Take this blue one 'ere." And simultaneously points as he rides on.

Old Jim Pickens oversees the whole escapade through his thick lensed specs, making sure all are mounted before he commits to join in at the back of the pack.

A sturdy pony is chasing the herd. Danny loses no time, takes probably his one and only chance and throws himself at the mare. He lands flat, chest on mane and is quick to realise she has no halter, or indeed any reins. The others now untangle from their cluster and the big horses lead out onto the peninsula first. The wide grassy ground juts out into the calmly lapping sea. The sun rises magnificently and with great synchronicity now begins to warm the bay.

It is a procession, everyone and everything instinctively joins in. The row of horses are joined by curious goats looking for new things to eat, and the dogs are having a great day, even the chickens and the bantams seem to decide it's an occasion. Each animal follows the other, safety in numbers or just up for the craic? A few mums are left at the back, maybe a little jealous but smiling, as they hold onto their babies and toddlers, relishing the unfolding spectacle.

There are ten or more riders, Danny can't look up to count. His mare is feisty and is kicking up a fuss. He talks to her; he is close, clinging onto her mane, knees tucked into her flanks.

"Come on now, easy as you go... look, I'm Danny, it's OK, we're gonna be OK, let's do this together." The rider introduces himself as the young mare can't decide if it's a rodeo or a jock. He tries to sit up, long mane hairs grasped between his fingers, she bucks, she rears. Animals melodramatically neigh at each other, part-excitement, part-fear. Some of the lead stallions rise up on hind legs at the front, their riders deft but only just in control. But not our Danny, as his bucking bronco does her best to shake him off. At the back of the parade it's a bumpy old ride. He *is* used to it, he *can* handle it — but she is giving him a really hard time — he leans his full body weight forward, again, as the mare rises up once more.

Brendon is the first one in. The heavy horse, shin deep in sea water, navigates between the stones and the sand. They don't seem to like it - this first bit; trepid, reluctant, but they go for it once they are in. It's not long before Brendon's horse is submerged into the water and so is he, to about waist deep. Holding its neck out long, the stallion's eyeballs are protruding and white, nostrils flared and teeth showing in a weird grimace. It now doggy paddles in that peculiar way horses swim. To come off at this stage could be lethal for a rider. To fall into the back hooves of a beast of this size whilst swimming is potentially deadly, by a kick to the head.

Now Mikey manages to coerce his stallion into the sea, soon joined by Trivet Dave, then Jim Pickens and all the rest soon follow. It is the grandest of sights. A sea of horse's heads bob about the bay.

Meanwhile our Danny is still struggling at the back. Even more compromised now. This strange blue mare led by her instincts has followed the pack, but really does not like the look of the water. Danny is having a hard time, part-laughter, part-frustration, mainly fear - but his dignity still intact, just about. And with the sheerest of determination our hero leads the horse to water. She tentatively steps in. But not without a final buck and rear. Danny loses his knee hold and is not quite sure how he has managed to cling on. He lies almost flat upon her back, as she rises on her hind legs. But then she is in, all of sudden and swims. The frantic mania now astonishingly replaced by the weightless buoyancy of the sea. As if stepping out of a wind tunnel, all around is suddenly and abruptly peaceful. The pair float admirably... but only momentarily. It does not last long!

Just as Danny had finally managed to persuade his charge that she would really like a dip in the sea, the rest of the crew have already had their wash and now begin racing back towards the camp. The thunderous rumble of heavy hooves on sandy grass pumps by. And Danny's mare is straight out of the water and starts chasing for her life after the rest of the herd.

A long narrow strip of charging beasts break into gallops along the peninsula and race towards the camp. Goats scatter and bleat, chickens flap and squawk. And one bucking horse and rider follows sporadically at the rear.

Coming in last, riding a blue pony, behaving more like a spring lamb than a horse, Danny finally catches up with the rest. He is hysterical with laughter and terror synonymously. And now the halted others watch the last horse finish – everyone is exploding with amusement; tears, roars and jeers all-round.

"She only just come off Connemara Moor!" Shouts Trivet Dave with hilarity.

Danny is instantaneously stern and straight-faced. It all happened too fast to sink in, but he gets it now. He looks to Old Jim Pickens, as appealing to referee:

"You're still young enough to bounce." Old Jim concedes.

Danny slowly joins the laughing, relieved to have gotten back home intact and promptly jumps off the young mare and sets her free – once more.

Mutation

The entrance is held by leather and rubber clad guards. Gas masks, concertinaed tubes, ghastly make-up and someone with what looks like a black handbrake cover from a truck - adorned as their preferred headwear of choice. This is not a bondage party, but some other class of out-there scrapyard freakery.

Guilders are exchanged for stamps on the backs of hands as Bonzo, Lacy, and Dave eagerly squeeze their way through the pack and into the immense warehouse.

There is already a sizeable crowd just mingling; it is still relatively early. The trio are momentarily stationary as they scan the enormity of the interior. Solid chunks of hangar-sized walls dwarf the participants. Searchlights span the black and white content, an impression of a close encounter is held. In the middle of the longest wall, some few hundred feet long, is a car. An old black Cadillac of some sort, it is in both this room and the next. A hole has been smashed through the wall and the vehicle placed in the middle of the void, neatly in line with the partition. Its doors have been cut off and its interior now morphed into a cutch. The backseats remain and a table is emplaced along with a pair of facing chairs. Freaks lounge, sup, and smoke.

Bonzo approaches the dark, metal and chrome clad bar. Black scaff poles, obligatory skulls and spanners decorate the space. Cold, strong lagers are ordered. They're a good price too. The trio slouch and take in more of the scenario. Dull yet reverberating thuds emit from the adjacent building as if some mysterious factory is at work. There is anticipation in the air and Bonzo is keen to get on. Between the three of them they have little money but are eager to spend what they have. Bonzo promptly integrates and immerses himself amongst some locals, yet straight to the point and after the source. He is kindly directed and simply told to look out for the white hat.

By tilting his head to the others, Bonzo directs Dave and Lacy into the next room. I say room but walled expanse is more apt; the enormity of these premises cannot be underplayed.

The strobes, the broken beats and the concreted thud of huge bass-bins impress upon ones chest from a matte black sound system. Giants of rusted metal loom over the dancers.

Intermittent metallic sculptures linger in the space, animated by meandering lights. Nuts, bolts and old car parts reassembled into new lifeforms. Junkyard art. Two gigantean robots shoot thirty foot licks of flaming fuel above the spectacle. The last drips of liquid fire extinguish before ground-fall, just above the crowd. Despite the palpable cyborgism, the night has a distinctly Dickensian feel. Perhaps it is the cold. This late October night – far out in these empty flatlands.

The trio gawp in impression. It's a spectacle all right. The music is to their liking and the Euro-freak crew looks diverse yet intense. A night ahead is now here as the three push their way forward towards the source of the sounds. Dreadlocks swing against skinheads, crusties, punks and divas – they are all here. Bonzo stands tall and scans the crowd like a beacon. Heads bob, feet stomp, and despite the cold, the temperature here is rising. His scanner now locks onto the white hat. She cleverly and clearly stands out amongst the black-attired crowd. Plunging his way into the cluster, Bonzo now swims through the masses. His sights fixed on the solo big, floppy white hat – serious summer wear from decades before and from a season now long past. It takes some time but his size assists his persistence and finally the two meet face-to-face. He raises three fingers, she mouths one hundred and fifty. Him all dirty and dark, her all smiles and light. An exchange is quickly made. There is no looking over ones shoulder here. Bonzo wastes no time - drops, gulps and immediately does an about turn to Dave and Lacy. All three unite, raise their drinks and grin at what lays ahead.

And as if on cue the bpms raise the ante. The English, the Dutch, the Irish and the Germans and so on... all merge. Some remain distinct but there are no borders here. The outside has now joined those inside and the masses throb, grow and mutate into a singular form; a superorganism. Shouts, jeers and whistles amidst a glut of foreign languages all letting out what they feel. And into the night they collectively dance for their freedom.

The trio are certainly feeling it now as sweat appears on brows. Grins turn to gurns as each and every one bounces. The beats thicken, the 303s squelch ever more, and then it all explodes.

Sparks, flashes and smoke fills the stage as the sound of the system abruptly disappears. All that can be heard are the ungainly putters of a generator and the protests that are erupting from the just coming up crowd. It's a mob. It's an impending riot. And simply no sounds.

Technicians appear, apologies are made and a forlorn DJ makes a swift exit. They all can't quite believe it. But all is quickly replaced by a band. They are soft rockers, white trainers, leather jackets and floppy hair. What the fuck is this? As the gurns turn to growls, the band has an impossible mission as the crowd stand static, stare at each other, or simply retire to the bar.

Replenished by a new cold beer, Bonzo swaggers in dismay. The naff music cuts through. His whole existence is now seriously fractured as a distinctly odd atmosphere looms in the vast and now vacuous space. He stares down at his beer, alone and wandering. He stares twice at the floor. He looks again. Trick of the light or trick of the night? It is an arrow. Illuminated, UV. Yes, and another. Definitely, yep, them there are arrows. He grins to himself. Confused. Bemused. Simply focusing on the floor. What else do you do with an arrow on the ground... but follow it. And another. They are large and now distinct and lead out of the warehouse and towards a door. On a goofy mission with cold can in hand, Bonzo is happy to explore. He leaves the soft rock behind him.

He temporally stands in front of two massive hangar doors. Separated. Alone. He briefly looks up and down the twenty-feet of this vast exit. Eventually he decides to give one of the doors a push; with some considerable effort. It scrapes open slowly and he tentatively steps out into the unknown. And Whooosh! Jets of flame splash in front of his face and he jumps back in alarm. He can feel the heat on his flesh. His pulse abruptly increases. Inches away from a singeing, he quickly takes cover inside the building. He gives it a moment and peeks out once more from the cover of the warehouse door... and Whoosh! Another jet of liquid flame, this time a little further past him. The grinding sound of heavy machinery on concrete passes directly in front of him. The sudden heat of the fire now quickly replaced by the raw cold of the night. A fire-breathing beast lets out another shot from its slow, but deliberate, enormous mechanical jaws. The absolute darkness of the night is temporarily illuminated by the jet of orange flame. The spectacle clankers past as Bonzo watches a leather bound and masked rider who controls the creature from high above. The abstract machinery creaks off down the raised old track amongst metal and wooden derelict warehouse buildings.

It is a dense complex, and a stunned Bonzo attempts to clear his vision after a momentary blinding. In the now even darker darkness, he can make out row upon row of uniformed hangars. It appears as a vast concentration camp but he purposefully deletes this image from his mind. Another flare is let out lighting this black night and the original occupation of the beast is determined. It was at some point, somewhere, in a former life - a combine harvester.

With the coast clear Bonzo follows the spectacle and steps out onto the track and notices further arrows pointing in the same direction as the beast. He saunters onwards between warehouses. A distant fire can be seen.

On closer inspection a Dutch Bill Sykes warms his hands around a raging oil drum fire as he chats to his old mate, Fagin.

The scenario is distinctly dystopian. An insane bull terrier, probably named Bullseye, ravages an old railway sleeper. It disturbs Bonzo. His recent attendance and facial expression distracts the others' conversation temporarily. The heavily accented and nonchalant response does nothing to appease Bonzo and even less so in taming the dog with its mouth full of splinters. Bonzo shakes his head to try and clear it again and is keen to move on.

The sound of live music is distant, almost non-existent, as is the trundle of heavy machinery. He looks to the skies. Crystal clear, twinkling for sure – no moon and all stars. However, it's a momentary moment of admiration, as fears of loss seep in. Where is he? Amongst the uniform wood and steel, each with their own alleys, a grid – a maze. Mood changed, Bonzo searches all that he can see – and hear. It's OK – an orange glow to the west, which must be Amsterdam, the soft tones of rock music far away behind him; but a new and faint sound ahead attracts him. On he presses. Irregular arrows confirm the way.

This new music is becoming increasingly distinct, but deceptively evasive as to its source. The jaws of Bonzo begin to grind once more as his shoulders start to bob in time to his stride. Curiosity continues to fill our wanderer.

Finally, the way-markers lead into one of the many warehouses and further into the dark and the unknown. It's like a fun-house at the fairground, but in the early hours amongst abandonment. Not forgetting his whereabouts – Bonzo tentatively immerses himself into the pitch-black. Hands raised around his head, almost anticipating a clunk to his back, fists clenched – a shadow boxer, but only really scared of himself.

A few steps forward and the gloom is transient as a steep wooden staircase can now be made out. And, of course, arrows of welcome are on each step. The beats from above now confirm he is in the place to be. But a staircase? Perhaps best described as a significant ladder that only seems to lead to a roof. But at its zenith it becomes clear, with a good push - it's a trap-door.

Bonzo is in the middle of a dance floor, only waist-high. Watching raving feet in strobe lights and looking at flickering legs with delight. This is the real party. Deep, down and dirty. Some of the legs, Bonzo notices, are fine and exposed. Feeling lucky, he smirks to himself. Our intrepid explorer has discovered El Dorado.

He locks eyes and grins and slips into auto-flirt with a gorgeous dancer above. Hands lean down with smiles and invitation. His dreamy animation is interrupted as larger men shout, "Close za fockin' door".

Trap-door shut and dancing shoes on, feet involuntary spring in time to the tunes. Bopping, yet surveying, he looks around the beautiful crowd. It's much warmer in here. Everyone is wearing less. Everyone stares back in grins, words mouthed under the volume of music, collective "Yahs" are exchanged. There are a few hundred people in here and they look like they have been partying for some time. This must be an inner-sanctum, an in-the-know zone. Shortly afterwards, they are joined by even more revellers seeping through the floor. The party ranks swell.

Strung up above in the intricate and hefty wooden eaves, are huge cargo nets. The under carriages of party goers, snogging couples and bouncing boys can be seen.

The mutants are here. A few are on the peripheries of the dance floor mounting themselves on Mad Max motorbikes. Our raver dances and stares, confused at the sight but not concerned. Altered states and fast lighting do not give a clear picture as the pirate bikers set off amidst the crowd. Despite their full-size, these trial-style, trash-junk motorbikes appear to float. Certainly no petrol engine is used in here. Are there devices underneath? Bonzo guesses, maybe battery power? He can make out rings on the front of the machines around the headlights – strange adaptations for sure. White sheets of satin start to billow and take form. Balloons. Big sacks of gas fill out from the front of the motorbike machines. Increasing in size, the bikes gently drift to the centre of the dance floor. Dancers in ecstasy: eyes closed; bodies twisting; hands making shapes in the air. The mutants aim straight for them. Their inflated, silken balloons are now fully enlarged, stretching a few feet high and round. Enough to gently engulf and smoother the high-flyer on the dance floor. Arms flap and hands swirl as the hedonists climax in delight. The tactile experience seems to carry them further; angels writhing in clouds.

Bonzo wants to stay up forever but his legs eventually begin to tire. He explores the space further, takes water, nods at sweet faces and stares up at a rope ladder. It's the cargo nets. Once containing tanks or jeeps dropped from a Herculean aircraft they are currently occupied by party people.

Whence the top is reached, he dismounts the ladder. Below the tautest corner sags a seemingly distant net and, as if immersing oneself into a pool, he lets go. It's tempting to plunge but easy to bounce and collide so Bonzo lowers himself with ease. Yet he soon loses control: forward and down onto his knees and into a roll speedily finding the lowest point. Sharply but awkwardly sitting up, he has found his spot at the base of the net. His fingers clasp the strands of the cargo net as he tries to get himself the right way up. And to the sweetest surprise he is met with the nicest of smiles. They don't share each other's language but not before long they share each other. And the night soon turns into day.

The Road is Foggy

Alarms sound, a heavy metal triangle is clanked, as an antiquated World War Two air-raid siren slowly winds to a crescendo; once again filling the atmosphere of the East End.

Freaks, residents, recruits, and an assemblage of all sorts run backwards, forwards, up and down - in every possible direction. Slim Bob and Natty Padlock sit, almost motionless, in the frenetic commotion on beaten old sofas and roll fags.

"'Ere we go again," mumbles Natty nonchalantly; an underplayed response to the emergency around him. "They always do this, give out false alarms to wear us down and try to catch us out," adds Slim Bob as an aficionado of such bizarre scenarios.

Like two lazy builders on a Monday morning, they both light their roll-ups and concede that indeed maybe an actual eviction is about to occur and they better get up onto the rooftops before it's too late. Natty scrolls his black woolly hat to and fro in some sort of ritualistic practice before rubbing his face. Slim Bob sports long blonde dreadlocks under a black baseball cap, but when lifted, reveals a bonehead underneath. He scratches his head stubble before replacing the cap/wig. This simple double persona has served him well on his actions during these summer months. There had been many spies and a detective agency but as the court papers had proven, a simple hairy hat had been effective enough to divide Slim Bob into at least two.

The veterans drag their weary torsos upright and proceed. The eager have been locked into position for some time as Natty and Slim Bob are some of the last ones to clamber onto the rooves before the ladders are finally drawn up. Many up there are bright-eyed, bushy-tailed and face-painted. There is an air of excitement and anticipation; however our two lads have an air of underwhelment. They straddle the tiled ridge of the roof with expressions as though they had been long awaiting a bus to come. Hands tucked into pockets, elbows straight, and chins tucked against the cold; thoroughly unimpressed by the inconvenience of probably the biggest eviction this country has ever seen.

They had been hard at it; they were always hard at it. Partying all weekend, barricading and defending for weeks now, following a whole summer of digger diving and crane climbing – and now this was it! But they were both so tired now.

As the final street party came to its conclusion at the weekend, the lads were still working away. The hundred foot tower of scaffolding, which burst through the end of the terrace house, had had its final poles secured into its punk style construction. It had been spray-painted all fluorescent pink and lime green. A bizarre and elaborate watchtower that now looked out for miles around this East End.

Around midnight on Sunday night, it was decided one final instalment was needed. Sounds.

They were all clustered by the fire, slumped on the sofas in the street, when the ever animated Scouse turned up with two big speakers and insists on their emplacement – on top of the tower. They all groan.

"How the fuck are we gonna get those up there?" pleads Slim Bob incredulously.

After a moment of ponder Scouse returns with a big knife and turns to the burnt-out car next to the fire. The abandoned motor had been rolled into the street a few weeks before and filled with concrete and scaffold poles and sprayed with obligatory colours - KerPlunk style! Scouse clambers through the driver's door and slashes out the seat belts and returns to the fire pit.

"Easy!" he proclaims, as he now secures a seat belt to one of the speakers, promptly hauls it onto his back and straps it on. The dreadlocked giant indicates to Slim Bob to do the same. Slim Bob sighs.

Retrieving the last of his energy, Slim Bob struggles with the heavy load and using all the strength from his knees to stand up straight, he looks up at the immensity of the tower and gulps at the thought of ascending once more the humongous and ridiculously precarious clamber. Like everything on the street nothing is straightforward. This tower is not a simple construction with an obvious route up, it has been built by the deranged. The ascent is far from common sense; part-deterrent — part-haste.

On the first steps of the ladder Slim Bob experiences the heavy weight of the speaker pulling him backwards and the straps instantly cut into to his skin through his many layers of clothing. Once on the roof, he buckles his belt tighter around his thick old sheepskin coat but what one gains in resistance to the discomfort of the cumbersome loads, is lost to a sudden rise in body temperature. He looks up. It is a long way up. Realising his precarious state, underfed and overdosed, the head spins as reason takes over his chemistry. You can do it. Yes you can. He pushes himself into the first frames of the eccentric structure, concentration overrides fear as each and every pole is negotiated. He looks like a turtle trying to climb a tree. But, as they say, the only way is up, baby.

Slowly climbing, twisting, circumnavigating a lengthy route; straight-up is not option. Spurred on by Scouse's continuous rant, insane laughter and perpetual enthusiasm from above – onwards and upwards they go. The polluting breeze of the East End begins to swirl smog as they gain some altitude. The scene is lit by industrial scale lighting in place for the imminent eviction. The light helps, but also adds impressionism to the surrealistic situation. A glowing drizzly gloom. The Grove Green road is now in full view, van loads of slumbering cops and guards line the street. All is quiet on this Sunday night cum Monday morning.

Eventually a platform within a cage is met, this will feature heavily in the forthcoming eviction – but for now, all is still.

Scouse unloads his speaker, sits down and pulls out two tins of red stripe from his pockets and laughs randomly and manically as Slim Bob readily accepts refreshment. The discarded weighty load of the speakers now make the lads feel as light as ever. That, mixed with the heady height and a euphoric sense of achievement means all is temporally well.

It is short-lived.

"Right, now all we need is the amp and cassette deck." Slim Bob sighs once more, aware that the clamber needs repeating. In recompense the second run will, at least, be lighter.

They continue their endeavours late through the night, hauling equipment, cables and connections – up and down the tower they go. By the time they are nearly finished, the reluctant and shy, early winter daylight emerges through the dirty old town's grey blanket. It is the very early hours by the time the last of the connections are made. The first of the workers can be seen way down below, back down there in reality – pedestrians commence their Monday morning commute.

Through a bag of tapes Scouse searches until he is certain to find the right tune. Power on. Lights glow on top of these hundred feet up. Some call it the Tower of Power others affectionately have named it 'Dolly', in respect for the 93 year old lady who had lived on the street all of her life, remaining resident and defiant until the latest opportunity possible.

So far down below even Claremont road is as quiet as it ever gets. From the psychedelic chaos on one side of the terrace, the view allows the rest of normality to be seen and of course, the miles of open scar can be viewed all around. The incumbent road spreads from the east, eating houses and trees and once green parks, now just mud.

This is one of the few hours in the week where a near silence is present. Soon the first planes of the day will take off and the over-ground tube trains begin.

There is hush, then there is...

HALLELUJIAH Hallelujah, Hallelujah
We're here to pull ya
Back in to do it all the same
Hallelujah, hallelujah
Not sent to save ya

Just here to spank ya n'play a game

The Happy Mondays aptly break the silence and can be heard for miles around. The odd startled commuter breaks from their dreary trance to attempt to source the sound. Scouse and Slim Bob celebrate with another Red Stripe and do a Bez rave on the small platform.

Back on the roof-tops Natty Padlock and Slim Bob debate the possibility that this actually might finally be an eviction for real. Through the tree houses, across the rail track and far off into the cemetery, masses of media can be seen assembling. Huge white television cameras can just about be spotted preparing and taking position. Word is out that this is as close as the cops are going to allow them. It's a joke. For so long Claremont Road had been a stronghold, a defiant gesture to the monopoly players, it was ours! But as the truth sinks in that the media have been sectioned so far away in the distance, the vulnerability of this alternative community permeates all those ready to resist. After all, the media are one of the few forms of protection they have from the full force of the state.

"Fuck, I didn't get to put on any socks!" Slim Bob looks down at his ankles, already shading blue. They don't know how long they are going to be up here, some have it planned for possibly weeks. He tucks himself deeper into his old button-less '70s football manager's style sheepskin coat, tied in with a thick leather belt.

"Fuck, I still got these!" Natty Padlock retrieves a few incriminations from the small pocket in his jeans. Without hesitation he licks one like a stamp, swallows and laughs at Slim Bob. With some reluctance, but acceptance Slim Bob follows suit.

The late afternoon drags on. It is otherwise an unremarkable, November grey day. The initial momentum wanes as those eagerly locked-on begin to feel a little impotent and others begin to grumble like kids on a long bus journey. There have been a few initial melees on the ground. A man in a wheelchair is aggressively manhandled, a few of the elderly are pushed and shoved, and a brave protester, neck deep at ground level, is slowly angle-grinded out of his lock-on. It is enough of a confirmation that this is the final push — but then all goes ominously quiet. As the receding autumn sun goes down, it becomes apparent to all, what the state of the state's play will be; by all accounts — they have opted for a nocturnal invasion.

It's a sinister twist and apprehension shows on many of the faces which are huddled under blankets, carpets and bits of old tarpaulin; anything to keep out the now entrenching cold.

As night falls, many are subdued but not Natty Padlock and Slim Bob. They are coming up. Their animation begins to twinkle. There is a lot to explore and the only way to stay warm is to move around. Their playground is an entire terrace of houses, all now one mass of intricate barricades.

They drop in for tea round at Speedy Bobs. His enclave is an intensely cramped attic space. He is excited to have guests; at this late stage, he is excited by everything. The entire space is not for the claustrophobic nor the clumsy. A partition wall and a forty-five-degree sloping roof space have been crammed full of spring loaded bicycle wheels and parts- a chrome slinky-dink zone of bewilderment. It has a huge trap door that slams him closed in, leaving just about enough space to sit cross-legged. It's insane, he's insane. As he twitches and strokes his 70's style drop handlebar moustache, he boasts that he can stay here for weeks. He is not too worried about food supplies but running out of his favourite sweeties might not be such a pretty sight.

Natty and Slim Bob wish him luck, finish their tea and move on. Both are impressed and surprised by the intricacy of the fortifications. Despite this tightly knitted community, much of the work has gone on in secret and there are many final installations to behold. One of the upstairs bedrooms has sensibly been stacked with firewood and now an entire roomful huddle around the fireplace. It is jovial and cosy, these barricades have been homes to many protestors for months now, even years to some of these residents. There is an informal pecking order of who gets closest to the fire.

"Just so you know..." a ginger dreadlocked and bespectacled Potty Bill wags a finger, conspiratorially encouraging the lads to follow him into an adjacent room. Unsure as to Bill's meaning, the two stand vacant in an empty and unremarkable former bedroom. Bill opens a wardrobe door. Slim Bob and Natty look at each other blankly, then look inside the wardrobe. They look in, look around, frown, one pushes the back of the wardrobe and looks at Bill. "There 'baint no Narnia 'ere?" Still not yet caught on - and then they both look down. It is bottomless. The outline of an oil barrel deftly fits into the space. A tunnel.

"It leads all the way to Grove Green Road... just in case you might need it!" winks Potty Bill whilst tapping his nose and grinning slightly.

The lads both dopily grin and nod as they take in the extent of this project. It must pass down through this house on Claremont, underneath two gardens and a terrace house on Grove Green Road. It ends in an ally's front room; remarkably kept secret all along.

The two move on, now more animated and excited than before. All begins to glimmer and twist. This has become an adventure, exploring what has been there all along. They have travelled the rooftops and the upper floors but the ground floors remain vacant for obvious reasons.

They acquire some climbing rope along the way.

"Let's drop into the café," suggests Natty. And so a barricade is temporally lifted as the pair now ponder a deep, dark space below. It is too risky to use their head torches but they push each other on into the dark. Aware that they will only be a door or a window's breadth apart from the Babylon, the adrenalin and sense of mischief spurs them on. Slim Bob goes first and tentatively dangles for a moment as the acoustic changes upon entering the roof space of the empty café. He can hear activity now out on the street, something they had both been unaware of for some time. Machinery, footsteps and low guttural growls of instruction from the cops and the security guards that are out there but unseen. Slim Bob's heart beat raises. Should he be doing this? He is committed now. Like a black clad jewellery thief in a Bond movie he expertly lowers himself gently to the floor. His feet softly connect. He moves quickly and quietly to the nearest wall and finds a shadow, one eye on the door and window all the time. Natty soon follows and joins him.

Acclimatising, the trick of closing one's eyes and counting to thirty, now enables them to see better in the dark. They both observe the scene. This dark and abandoned space was once the heart of the street - a busy café churning out cheese toasties and cups of tea all day and night. A huge mural of a smoking Bob Marley smiles and oversees them; once residents, now intruders. Tony, the Frosties Tiger, grins at them with a spanner in his hand.

They both love the excitement, naughty is after all their nature. However, they both silently look back at the single rope and know that if it comes on top, only one will get away - if they are lucky.

Intrepidly, Slim Bob approaches the old fridge as Natty rushes with a raised hand and silently interrupts his action. Without words he points to the plug in the wall; to open the fridge would illuminate the whole proceedings and give their game away. The power down here may or may not still be on but it's not worth the risk. He quietly unplugs it and Slim Bob opens the door safely. Sitting central on the shelves of the retired fridge sits a huge bowl of trifle and four tins of red stripe. They laugh without sound to themselves. Someone's little gift to the explorers, attention to detail throughout this entire encampment will be its epitaph.

With the bowl cuddled under Slim Bob's arm, the pair scoff cream and custard with their hands. The lagers are stuffed in their pockets for later. They step forward in confidence to further explore the dark and vacant space. Ghostly echoes of former frenetic times fill the void. Already nostalgic, this space will be greatly missed by them. Slim Bob steps up to the barricaded door with gusto but stops suddenly, as cracks of light shine through. He has little view but positions himself so he can see from around a corner, as if hiding from gunfire. He stops eating the trifle, not quite believing what he can see.

They had grown used to the pigs, the cat and the mice, and the run-ins since Thatcher's boot boys had shown their psychosis at the Beanfield, the Poll Tax Riots and the more recent melees that followed. But up until then they were old Keystone cops with awkward tit helmets on their heads, which often fell off. Small, round, Romanesque shields were all they had to protect themselves as they went in for their charge. But what is this that now looms in the doorway with its back turned to the door? Slim Bob takes another ghastly peek through the gap in the old café door. The robot clads its neck with a black material covered metal brace; it pulls on gloves that reach to the elbow, also weighted and metallic. The machine towers all in black. Judge Dread. Boots strapped knee-high. Finally the cyborg fixes his helmet, SP23 twinkles fluorescent in the street lights. Slim Bob had never seen the likes. The Special Patrol Group has now been consigned to history; welcome to the Tactical Support Group - the now notorious TSG.

It is only a door's width away, the darkness, the beast. Inside all colour, community and love; outside all hate. It is time to retreat as the foulness permeates their souls.

Time to revisit the roof and it sounds like the show has begun.

They can hear the Prodigy booming from the tower through the roof tiles above. Music for a jilted generation. They push their way through the small gap and re-enter the atmosphere. *Break and Enter* is playing, its sound effects of smashing and breaking glass are echoed by bailiffs now in the early hours beginning their worst. Tiles fall off the roof at the far end of the terrace as the darksiders start to tear their way in.

"We are more possible than you can powerfully imagine", gets shouted out followed by abstract cries of "Pie and mash".

The whole rooftop is raving, shouting and jeering. There are hundreds of people spread over thirty houses or more: tree houses, connecting cargo nets and, of course, the mighty tower.

This midweek, late November night is bouncing. Whistles blow, horns blare and arms are raised as the defiant dance the night away. The nocturnal spectacle is immense.

The invaders have logically started coming in at the end of the street, underneath the tower. The barricades hold them back for some time but they are hard at it, doing their worst: smashing, bashing and trashing – they are after all, destroyers.

The party is quickly cut short as the music suddenly stops. Whistles, shouts and moans fill the temporary quiet. The last splutters of a generator can be heard. The mood quickly flattens as the bailiff spoils the party. One nil to them.

It's a short-lived interruption, as some bright spark had obviously thought this one through... and it's not long before the music returns, louder than ever before. Rave on. A quick equaliser in the score. A second generator had been stashed higher up and the party continues with ever greater intensity. The volume goes up even further still.

What we are dealing with here is a total lack of respect for the law...

A timely intro-sample speaks out, as a dirty guitar and acid waves traverse the next track and soon breaks into full throb.

The atmosphere is as ecstatic as it is surreal. Strobe lit, nostrils flared, animalistic.

Fuck 'em and their law...

Then they come for the nets. A digger slowly and ominously rolls onto the street, its caterpillar tracks grinding and rumbling as it comes. As lonely as it is menacing. Beast like, yet stiffly mechanical.

The terraced houses run parallel with a row of mature trees which in turn follow the sidings of an overland railway track. The gap between the trees and the houses is the street's width and these aerial spaces have been filled by a succession of heavy duty cargo nets. Once utilised to deploy heavy military equipment dropped from helicopters, they are now being filled with defiant protestors.

People are screaming and shouting, "Protect the nets!" It has become obvious this is where they need to clear first. The invaders have to get their assaulting machinery into a clear location to attempt an assault on the rooftops and eventually tackle those in the tower.

Slim Bob dives off the roof with full trust in the construction. Not a swan dive, rather more of a bomb, as if into a swimming pool. He sinks and lightly bounces as he rolls somewhat out of control, momentarily. He is not safe in the seat of the net and quickly clambers up the face to a higher ridge point. There are foot soldiers amassing below. His throat lumps as he can now see the eyes of the robots just a few feet beneath him. He is close enough to hear their jeers and insults. School boys, bullies – not the brightest of sparks. They have new toys as well as their latest fancy dress. They taunt Slim Bob with their state-of-the-art technology, a carbon fibre extending telescopic baton, only having recently moved on from wooden clubs.

The cops below remain dormant for now as Slim Bob secures a more comfortable position. He has a full length view from the middle of the street. Straight ahead at the far end is old Dirks' house - a gallows pole and noose perched on its roof, a darkly artistic threat. And from around the corner, under full floodlight comes Babylon's beast and stretches up into the first net. Screams and roars can be heard coming from those closest to the action. Slim Bob adjusts himself to try and get a better view. They are up to something sinister, as can be heard by the cries in the vicinity, but it still remains unclear from this end of the street to exactly what they are up to. And then Slim Bob gets the picture. They are cutting someone out of the net from below. The protestor's full weight has been rolled into the centre of the cargo net which is now dangling thirty feet or more above the street. It's a girl and they are beating her in full view of hundreds around. She screams.

The seat of the net has been cut and they are violently trying to lower the victim from its web. Like a billiard pocket snipped at its base, a hefty snooker ball is ready to drop. A digger arm has been drawn up to meet the emerging protestor.

Then she drops.

Violently – thirty feet to the tarmac below.

A thud and then she is completely still.

Then there is silence.

Screams follow; roars and horror erupt. This couldn't have been in more plain view. Is she dead? This is not simple state violence, this is a simpleton's lack of brains. What were they thinking? The fury and disbelief explode as people are screaming and crying out the girl's name. She remains motionless.

It takes an excruciatingly long time before medics and a stretcher appear. She is eventually manoeuvred. There are signs of movement and confirmation from the ground that she is still alive. It is later discovered that she had smashed her pelvis, amongst other serious injuries in the preventable fall.

It is not long before the net she had occupied is cleared and cut down. The beast below continues further on up the street. As Slim Bob watches he quickly stirs. His net is slunk over hefty ropes, pulled taught from roof to tree. This is what holds all of the nets up. A posse of bailiffs have sneaked an extension ladder under his net and lean it against the tree. At the top of the ladder a boiler suited agent unexpectedly appears. A glinting knife is seen in the darkness as he promptly begins to cut into the supporting rope.

They are going to kill me, Slim Bob realises. He looks quickly from tree to rooftop and back again. Assessing that he has just a few seconds before they cut the rope and his net would quickly swing and plummet with his full body weight. It does not take much of a calculation to see he will smash straight into the brick wall of a house, twenty feet or more below. Rapidly, out of nowhere, an athletic elder appears. Armed solely with a wooden walking stick held the wrong way around. He remarkably manages to run the taut length of the supporting rope. A tight-rope walker, well runner, just once or twice maintaining his balance with the crook of his stick. He swoops in on the bailiff with strike after strike. First the knife flies out of his hand, followed by quick swipes from the walking stick to the bailiffs' hands and then his helmeted head. It is a swift retreat. Time enough for Slim Bob to scramble back out of the net and onto the roof. The defender only left with dwindling twines to support him before he deftly leaps into an adjacent tree house.

Safely back on the roof and Slim Bob has had enough. He slips through a gap back into the solace of one of the top floor rooms to recover and retch.

The following days grind on slowly with a brick-by-brick dismantling of the street. Protestors are picked off one by one as supplies and energy are drained. Each and every one will have their own stories of this - the longest eviction in recent British history, defiant to its end. The state was always going to get its way, everyone knew that. They must be proud of the now thirteenth largest traffic jam in the country. As the temperature and the sea rises around the world and the smog thickens, you can't help but say "we told you so."

And so it goes on...

There is no drama left for Slim Bob and Natty Padlock, simply exhaustion, a come down and intense hunger. The cold sets in further. The grey, dank London sky permeates them entirely.

Grumpy Steve appears in a similar low-spirit yet inadvertently reveals that it is his giro-day.

"Full-English all round, is it then?" Slim Bob retorts with breakfast on his mind. And the three bold defenders, without theatrics, climb down a ladder and walk off the end of the street. Simple.

The eviction has created a significant number of displaced people, now without homes. Old Dirk and crew had pre-empted this by squatting a local, disused dairy. It was all about capacity and vicinity, pragmatic yet a stark contrast to the glories of Claremont Road. What once, until recently, had been a colourful and thriving community, is now confined to a sombre barrack. The bleak and vacuous space is filled with rows of military hospital-style beds with those thin grey blankets to add to the sense of institution. Everywhere stinks of gone-off milk.

The injured, exhausted and bewildered are all crammed in with far too many dogs, who are also without a street to run free in. Old Dirk does his best to accommodate the latest arrivals but space has almost run out. He points to a far corner and shows Slim Bob that there is one bed left for him. Without possessions, just the stinking clothes he now stands in, he moves towards the symbolic place of rest. A dog has shat right in the middle of the blanket on top of the bed. Slim Bob does not hesitate, swivels on his heels, and immediately does a U-turn.

Lost, confused, and disorientated to time and place – Slim Bob wanders back outside, down the street and back towards the eviction.

The early evening gloom has set in as spotlights now are fixed to illuminate the tower. Cherry pickers rise and attack at various points on the way up. Slim Bob joins a cordoned crowd of onlookers on Grove Green Road. The eviction is now five days and nights in and will take a few more before it is all over.

"Power to the Tower!" Shouts the crowd. There are cops everywhere. Two or three rows thick in places. Some have been here for all these days and nights and they have lost the sense of humour that they never had. Amongst the jostle Slim Bob can see a known and allied reporter, a photographer. When his flashes momentarily stops, they both greet and briefly chat and Slim Bob soon leaves with a donated tenner in his pocket. Straight into the next door pub.

Quite suddenly, numbed by the muffle of the chaos outside, Slim Bob sheepishly approaches the bar. Here is the dour and the miserable having nothing whatsoever to do with the commotion outside of the door. Workers drown their sorrows, each mainly meditating in solitary over clasped pints. A few other protestors are quiet in corners, ones which neither Slim Bob recognises nor knows. He takes his pint and sits alone.

And then another pint. And then less a sense of wellbeing, more a notch above feeling totally shit. Anaesthetically speaking things have improved. But Slim Bob's blur, fatigue and advanced state of dissolution provoke fractured thoughts. Sleep. He needs sleep. He wants to be away from here. On a tropical island with gin and tonics, but this is the East End. No palm trees here.

No money left. Slim Bob swings open the doors of the pub where the volume of the generators and jeering crowd enters his presence once again. He has a plan, maybe not a good one, and runs straight into a line of defending coppers. As full as he can muster he takes them on in their mass. "Come on then!" No fists or boots, a mere scarecrow tumbling into their arms. And not before long and Slim Bob is in the back of the van, now surrounded by the ugly faces of the Met.

"You selfish scum, do you know how much this is costing the tax-payer?" "Do you know how much you fucking stink?" Slim Bob is silent, doubled over, looking them all straight in the eye with his bloodshot pair. He does not give a fuck. He does not need to explain. He will not give them the pleasure and smirks as they do their worst. It's not long before they have rounded up some more and back to the station they go.

A bed, a cell – it's the Hilton to Bob as the sergeant unlaces his boots and takes them away along with his belt. "I don't need an alarm call." These are Slim Bob's last words before he rolls over into the best of deep sleeps.

A duty solicitor wakes Slim Bob at some point in the night, reads out his charges, but neither really care.

Come the next morning the cell door is opened. "Right – you're out. No charges."

"Leave me alone, I just need more sleep."

"Leave me alone… " Slim Bob offers a contented mumble. He rolls over, pulls the blanket ever tighter over his head and returns, momentarily, to his greatest luxury in weeks.

Merry-go-round

She awakens. Head a little sore, throat and mouth dry - but salvageable. She lays in her bed and can hear the rough, parched roars of the night watch, just about to call it a morning. Barely comprehensible, but some dispute over nothing and then fades. Dogs bark.

Maggie arises and gets the fire going easily. She puts the kettle on the trivet and assesses the situation around her. Another more conscious early riser is bagging up dented and discarded gold brew tins from around their camp. A few sleepy children appear, long jumpers, no trousers and coloured wellington boots with bowls of porridge in their hands.

This was one half of the convoy that had been separated the night before. They had hoped they would be on top of Twmbarlwm by now, as they had been this time last year. But the state was having none of it and had intercepted them with full force the afternoon before. Blockades on the motorway, a slow-go corral and despite enthusiastic defiance, they had managed to break the group into at least two, maybe more. Tedious hours had been spent the previous day, contained on the hard shoulder, less than five miles-per-hour all the way. The helicopters had tried to track them, but most of the old buses and trucks had angled their wing mirrors at ninety degrees and it gave them some respite from the harassment from above. The tactic worked perfectly well on that sunny June afternoon, jubilant shouts of *"Pigs in space"* went out; so they gave-in for the day and flew home.

Maggie is joined by Tracker John, to come and share the now ready tea. He had been tuned into the shortwave radio and had managed to pick up the Gwent police communications. John's approach was militaristic. He unfolds his ordnance survey map on the ground and uses small stones to hold down each corner. The others were at least six miles away. Maggie was amused by his outlook, but equally grateful for his diligence. They both examined their surroundings, a rough, high sided quarry. They had arrived in the dark, just about room for all to squeeze in, but maybe not all. It was chaos; as usual. SNAFU. It was clear to them both that they could not stay here. Too steep, too rocky, much too exposed, and a high chance of stones falling down, or even worse, thrown.

John said a crew had been out in the night and found another site, an abandoned railway siding. It was a good one... but the Transport Police had anticipated its suitability and had their lackeys dump a few tons of debris in the entrance. However, John smirked, and indicated that this was not a problem, as their picks and shovels had already made a good dent:

"Just follow the green camper van when we are all ready." And with that he finished his tea and went about his mission to inform each and every one scattered around this literal pit-stop.

The Welsh morning air is fresh and the start of the day suggests it is going to be bright. On one hand she is disappointed that their mountain goal had not been met, fearing how much more aggressive the state's response had been. This was one of the first gatherings of the year. But she is equally comforted that elsewhere has been found and in the knowledge that they would all be together again by tonight; and this spurred her on. She continues to clear up, using the remaining hot water to clean the plates from last night's meal; it's bad luck to travel with washing-up, don't you know?

Maggie tats down. Making sure everything is secure. Plates, cups, and cutlery are all stashed in a box under the bed. Candles and books are put away. She briefly glimpses the interior of her beloved home, an old former telecom truck, now comfy and decorated; entirely different than its original occupation and indeed its former occupants. She makes the bed and glances a few old photos on the wall. Memories - good ones. She smiles.

As she gathers the last of her things from around the fire pit, a Super Vega bus attempts to start. The slow rotation of the starter clunks, over and over again. Rhythmical, but not dissimilar to a heavy smoker clearing their lungs. Once more the ignition is turned and hopes for the engine to fire are increased by promising sounds. Another series of goes and the engine rises like a reluctant old dog getting up from around the fire.

Maggie quickly slams her back doors shut and jumps into her cab, windows rapidly drawn, as the old bus begins to bellow deep, black smoke. At first it appears to fill its belly boxes, then the exhaust gains strength as the driver pumps the accelerator and plumes begin to fill Maggie's now redundant fire-pit. She loves the sound of the old buses, it purrs felinely as it ticks over. Another one fires up nearby.

She sits patiently, somewhat anxiously, alone in her cab and contemplates the day ahead. She can just about make out the road below and the outside world and hope things will go well. She admires the old Super Vega next to her, battered but bold. Its old blue and white paint work, now chipped and tarnished, but someone's treasured home. To her left she watches a biker she had met the night before, Ghandi she thinks he called himself, and she chuckles at his unlikely name. He now folds a tarpaulin and shoves it tightly into a sidecar of his jet black Norton. His leathers and denim are just as dark as the grease that covers his bike. His long, dank hair, his bald patch and his impressively long beard; Maggie imagines small animals living in there.

It takes a while and the quarry fills with the sound and the smoke of the anticipatory antiquated fleet; all are ready to disembark. And as if by magic there it is - the green camper van out on the road.

The Vega pulls out first, a Panorama coach next. Maggie waits her turn, as the convoy slowly uncoils from its night stop. Eventually she turns out onto the highway. She looks left, looks right and follows the bus in front. Everyone crawls to allow all to attach, no one gets left behind. It's a super organism, with no one in charge but works well as one. No cops today —yet— hopefully they are too busy in Newport or Swansea, but will probably show up at some point.

And not before long, they are all out on their way; wheels-a-turning, once again.

The half mile long convoy fills these back roads. Turns are made and inclinations increase, as the ascent into the hills is made. More smoke and less speed as the old vehicles chug on up. There is no one there to notice them and this spectacle; just a few sheep who are only interested in the grass before them. Maggie admires the late spring now turning into summer. Verdant hills nestle amongst each other, the south Welsh landscape very much unchanged. Desolate, open, just home to the woolly livestock and little else. The truly fine scenery, the green and pleasant land, just the low hum of the engines and all is well. That sense of freedom envelopes, as they all slowly proceed.

A small roundabout is approached and the bumper-to-bumper vehicles snail their way on. To their left an old black Hummer approaches, with a few vans and trucks behind it. It is Duke and crew in a recently acquired old car. It has been sunny, so they had decided to angle grind the roof off; the once saloon – is now an open-top classic. She can't quite see who is driving but Duke stands up in the passenger seat shouting and laughing; happy to have found the rest of the group. He wears white plastic sunglasses, probably suited better to a teenage girl but along with a cropped Afro-Mohican, looks punk as fuck.

Maggie's truck drops back to allow the latest to join in. In front the Hummer blasts out The Clash, the hills now alive to the sound. She can make out a fresh crate of brew on the back seat, as she watches the lads bounce with beer and nuttiness.

And further up into these hills they go. A half-hour of slow driving passes. Then another. This should not be taking so long? They all act on some kind of faith; plans and instincts kept at bay. Not wanting any unwanted information to be overheard or games to be given away. So far the cats have not shown up and so the mice trundle on their way.

But the roads now narrow into lanes and branches scrape along the sides of buses. Maggie stays cool, but doubt is definitely entering her mind. Safe in their numbers they proceed down another tight track. And so it goes on. They soon appear in the open again, as a left is taken at a small roundabout, and all can see the full spectacle unfold. Others have joined at the rear, some from the side, the convey is now over a mile long, but travelling at only just a few miles-per-hour.

Then it all slowly comes to a halt. Just stopped in the middle of a road. Air brakes press and hiss as handbrakes are pulled on tight. Engines steam with heat.

Maggie jumps out of her cab and walks briskly past the other buses, past the trucks and the Super Vega and then gets up to the front.

Two little old ladies have stepped out from a green camper van and now ask:

"Are you following us?"